THE
HEALTHY MIND
TOOLKIT

THE
HEALTHY MIND
TOOLKIT

**Simple Strategies to Get Out of Your Own Way
and Enjoy Your Life**

ALICE BOYES, PhD

A TarcherPerigee Book

tarcherperigee

An imprint of Penguin Random House LLC
375 Hudson Street
New York, New York 10014

Most TarcherPerigee books are available at special quantity discounts for bulk purchase for sales promotions, premiums, fund-raising, and educational needs. Special books or book excerpts also can be created to fit specific needs. For details, write: SpecialMarkets@penguinrandomhouse.com.

Library of Congress Cataloging-in-Publication Data

Names: Boyes, Alice, author.
Title: The healthy mind toolkit : simple strategies to get out of your own
way and enjoy your life / Alice Boyes, PhD.
Description: New York : TarcherPerigee, [2018] | Includes bibliographical
references and index.
Identifiers: LCCN 2017053507 (print) | LCCN 2017056018 (ebook) |
ISBN 9781524704537 (E-book) | ISBN 9780143130703 (pbk.)
Subjects: LCSH: Self-defeating behavior. | Cognitive therapy. | Mental health.
Classification: LCC RC455.4.S43 (ebook) | LCC RC455.4.S43 B69 2018 (print) |
DDC 616.89/1425—dc23
LC record available at https://lccn.loc.gov/2017053507

Printed in the United States of America

1   3   5   7   9   10   8   6   4   2

Book design by Elke Sigal

To Celeste—the best daughter a mother could hope for.

CONTENTS

....

PART 1

Understanding Self-Sabotage and Why We Do It

CHAPTER 1

. . . .

How to Use This Book

Welcome

. . . .

Have you ever experienced that feeling of exasperation when you realize you've created a problem for yourself? Maybe you stress yourself out over a request from your boss that turns out to be nothing, or you eat an entire family-size bag of popcorn because you didn't plan ahead while at the grocery store, or you turn down an opportunity because you're just not sure you can handle it. Whatever your situation, there's a common theme—you're getting in your own way.

In *The Healthy Mind Toolkit*, you'll discover the ways in which you're holding yourself back and how to leave that behavior behind. I'll help you escape from self-defeating traps so you can enjoy a clear, calm mind and more productivity, freedom, and resilience.

Together, we'll identify where you go wrong with your decision making. Then I'll help you put together a personalized toolkit of the skills you'll need for optimizing your thoughts and actions, which we'll tailor to your nature, lifestyle, and preferences. The result will be that you'll feel more relaxed, you'll sense your life is on the right track, and you'll have enough mental energy to withstand everyday stress and take on meaningful personal challenges.

The book is divided into five sections: understanding yourself, foundation skills, correcting thinking errors, relationships psychology, and finally, work and money. In modern life, most of us don't have any spare time or willpower for implementing ideas that are excessively complicated and exhausting. You need easy, practical solutions, which is exactly what you'll learn here. We'll work on both *knowing what to do* to achieve more of what you want and *how to do what you know,* so that you can successfully implement your insights and the book's tools.

Self-defeating behaviors are quite common, so you're certainly not alone in having this problem. And while each person's unique thought patterns and habits will be their own, there's a lot of overlap across people too. I can personally relate to many of the problem patterns we'll work through. In many cases, I've found simple solutions that work for me consistently. I've got strategies that prevent me from experiencing self-generated stress, or I can easily spot self-sabotage when I'm doing it and correct it on the fly. For example, I'm much better than I used to be at taking breaks, switching off my phone, prioritizing what I work on, seeing and implementing the simplest solutions to challenges, maintaining a balance between being cautious and carefree (preventing excessive worrying and ruminating), and not being penny wise but pound foolish.

In some cases, I find my self-sabotaging actions are harder to consistently prevent. I tend to react to change and surprises with anxiety-driven defensiveness. For example, a friend recently suggested she coordinate her vacation with my family's existing plans to visit a mutual friend of ours. My initial (internal) reaction was "Accommodating three sets of babies' nap schedules is going to be such a pain." However, I know myself well enough to spot this negative thinking as my typical first reaction to virtually *any* proposed change of plans. Sure enough, within a few minutes of thinking it over I realized the positives of all three of us getting together would far outweigh any minor scheduling and planning issues. My knee-jerk hesitation quickly shifted to feeling really excited about seeing both friends. Likewise, if someone makes an unexpected request of me, I often overestimate what the person is asking me to do. It's only later when I've stepped back and gotten perspective that whatever has been asked of me seems achievable and not a big deal (or even positive). When it comes to handling trickier requests (for example, being asked to do something I don't want to do), an easy compromise or alternative solution frequently seems obvious once I've had time to digest and process what has been asked. Although I have good insight into my patterns in this area, I don't always manage to hide my initial defensiveness at the time, and I sometimes need to go back and "clean up," apologize, or correct my attitude after the fact.

Ideally, using what you'll read here, you'll discover strategies for preventing your self-sabotaging behaviors from occurring. Realistically, you'll probably find yourself doing a mixture of prevention and treating the wound, as I do. You'll permanently solve some problem habits, but a few will remain works in progress. I'll help you learn how to respond constructively when these types of ongoing patterns occur, so you don't go spiraling into harsh self-criticism and rumination or blaming others unfairly. That way you can limit (or even reverse) any negative impact of your tendencies on yourself and your relationships.

Interestingly, many self-sabotaging patterns that look unrelated on the surface are actually two sides of the same coin. Here are some common examples. Can you relate to any of the following?

YOU:

Have too much chaos in your life, and not enough structure and routine.	◀▶	Stick too rigidly to self-imposed rules and routines.
Give up too soon.	◀▶	Persist too much.
Get excited and rush into action, without enough thought.	◀▶	Overthink and delay action because you never feel 100 percent sure.

Have a thinking style that's too optimistic. You focus mainly on the potential upside of actions and don't pay enough attention to potential problems.	◆▶	Have a thinking style that's too pessimistic. You shoot down good ideas, sweat the small stuff, and hold back from potentially wonderful opportunities.
Fail to reflect on and learn from past mistakes.	◆▶	Ruminate about the past and are prone to feeling excessive guilt and shame.
Have a "now" focus. You prioritize current wants at the expense of future well-being.	◆▶	Have a future focus. You deny yourself pleasure now in the hope of reaping rewards later.
Take too little responsibility. You have a tendency to blame others. You underestimate your control over your life. You hand responsibility over to others.	◆▶	Take too much responsibility. You overestimate your control over events and other people. You resist delegating.
Don't assert your preferences.	◆▶	Tend to dictate that others fit in with your terms, schedule, and preferences.
Have too little understanding of yourself and your nature. You do too little self-reflection.	◆▶	Have too rigid a view of your own nature. You do too much navel gazing.
Tend to underestimate how hard or time-consuming tasks will be.	◆▶	Tend to overestimate how hard or time-consuming tasks will be and fear them unnecessarily.
Underwork.	◆▶	Overwork.
Don't utilize small scraps of time effectively.	◆▶	Cram productive activity into any spare second, without giving yourself any true, guilt-free downtime.
Think too big.	◆▶	Think too small.
Don't care what other people think or the impact you have on others.	◆▶	Ruminate about what other people think.
Are prone to narcissism and overconfidence.	◆▶	Are prone to self-doubt and imposter syndrome.

Are too trusting of others.	◆➤	Are distrusting and suspicious. You have a negative expectation of others.
You avoid conflict.	◆➤	Never hold back from nagging or picking a fight.
Believe rules don't apply to you.	◆➤	Are too rule abiding. You don't recognize that rules often have hidden flexibility or gray areas.
Are too self-sacrificing.	◆➤	Are too self-centered and self-serving.

As you can see from the examples, there are many, many different self-defeating processes (some related to each other, some not). Even very widespread patterns don't manifest in exactly the same way for every individual. Rather than attempting to include every type of self-sabotage (which would fill a library rather than a single book), I'll provide simple, actionable tips for how to tackle the most common self-defeating patterns *and* teach you the principles behind these suggestions so you can adapt them for your precise needs. The more you customize the material from the book to address your specific habits, the better you'll understand it. And if anything you read here doesn't gel for you, feel free to ignore it. I'll give you plenty of options so you can choose what suits you best. By the end of the book, you'll have a set of specific solutions to apply in your life and a general toolkit for understanding your problem tendencies and successfully working through them.

The explanations and tips you'll read here are based mainly on cognitive behavioral theories and research. The term *cognitive behavioral* sounds formal, but it just means tweaking both your thinking and your behavior to have maximum positive impact. The dual emphasis is important because *changing your behavior tends to be one of the quickest and most effective ways to change your thinking.* A healthy mind starts with healthy behaviors, which is why this book includes many strategies that are focused on behavior, and why we'll concentrate in depth on the links between actions and thoughts. To truly declutter your mind, you'll need to streamline your behavior and switch out unconscious problem habits for more deliberate choices.

Cognitive behavioral approaches have been extensively studied, mostly as treatments for mental health difficulties. Decades of research have shown that cognitive behavioral strategies are a very effective approach for making emotional and behavioral changes.[1] Many common mental health problems, like anxiety and depression, include significant amounts of self-defeating behaviors, and these contribute to how people can get sucked into spirals of rumination (overthinking about the past), worry (overthinking about the future), and low mood. So although the book isn't specifically focused on alleviating mental health problems, if you have depression or anxiety, you can expect that the strategies I've included will be also helpful for those issues.

You Don't Need to Completely Eliminate Self-Sabotage

Your goal for using this book doesn't need to be to completely eliminate self-sabotage. In reality, that probably wouldn't be useful because life is so full of competing demands and wants and limited time and energy. A better goal is to identify and eliminate the patterns that are the most damaging to your health, happiness, and relationships. For example, putting off calling a friend isn't the same as putting off making a doctor's appointment after you've noticed a misshapen mole that could be a skin cancer. I'll help you figure out what's important to focus on minimizing and what's okay to leave as is. It's more critical to concentrate on the self-defeating behaviors that have the most harmful effects on you, rather than the frequency or number you do. By prioritizing the patterns that have the most significant potential consequences for you, you'll eliminate the majority of the negative impact that self-sabotage has in your life.

Goal Setting

A Catch-22 you may encounter as you progress through this book is that many self-sabotaging patterns also get in the way of overcoming self-sabotage. Great, right? Not prioritizing and trying to do it all is one example of this. To prevent this from happening, let's look at several different approaches you could take to prioritize the material in the book. Picking one of these options now will prevent you from trying to change all your self-defeating ways at once, becoming overwhelmed, and giving up.

> **Option 1:** Calculate what a good return would be from your investment in this book and set a specific, achievable goal to obtain that. For example, for the money you paid for it and the hours you spent reading it and absorbing the advice and suggestions, you'd like to identify and improve five self-defeating patterns.

> **Option 2:** If self-defeating patterns are having a big impact in only one domain of your life (for example, relationships or your career), you might choose to work through the material that relates to that domain thoroughly and read the rest of the book for interest, without the expectation of action.

> **Option 3:** If you're more motivated by taking a well-rounded approach, you might decide to implement one change in each of five life domains—general self-regulation, organization, relationships, work, and money. Or you might choose to implement one positive change from each chapter of the book.

Experiment

From the suggestions just given, identify your initial goal for reading *The Healthy Mind Toolkit*. What would you like to gain from applying the tips and strategies in your life? You can always pick further goals after you've achieved your primary objectives. If you set the bar too high initially, you'll end up feeling overloaded.

If you're worried you may not have the willpower to get through this book and *then* go back and start implementing the advice you like best, you can always pause when you reach an insight you want to apply in your life. Practice it until it's routine and then pick up where you left off in the book. This approach is likely to be particularly useful if you tend to be an "all research, no action" type of person.

Expect Your Insight into Your Patterns to Fluctuate

Before I became an author, I worked as a clinical psychologist in private practice in my country of birth, New Zealand. A pattern I observed was this: A client and I would spend a session untangling a specific problem. The client would seem to have gained insight into their pattern, and would leave the session feeling satisfied they'd acquired new understanding and tools. Fast-forward a few weeks, a month, or even the very next week, and the client would report a situation that was fundamentally the same issue that we'd worked through previously. However, to the client the situations seemed different. Therefore, it didn't occur to them to use the strategies they'd already learned in the new situation.

If you notice this happening to you, be aware that it's a known problem. It's not you, it's everyone. Frequently, it doesn't occur to us to translate insights and skills we've learned from one specific situation to other settings where they would be equally effective. In the moment, similar situations often seem completely distinct and unrelated to us. Sometimes it takes a while to get a really good handle on your repetitive patterns, but with patience, self-compassion, and perseverance, you'll get there. Expect the occasional face-palm moment when you recognize you've slipped into a familiar pattern you thought you'd resolved. You probably won't truly understand a pattern until you can think of at least ten different examples of how that pattern manifests in your life.

Even when your insights into your self-sabotaging patterns become ingrained, and you have a variety of strategies that work for you, you'll still have at least a few instances of falling into your old traps. The good news is once you're at this point, understanding what has happened and course correcting won't seem nearly as difficult or energy sapping as it felt initially. Using your strategies will become what you do automatically. When you notice you've repeated a familiar pattern it can even feel quite satisfying to whip out a solution you know works for you or simply realize you've identified the pattern and can react differently next time.

A Note on Ditching Harsh Self-Criticism

If you find yourself thinking, "That's me" in response to many of the patterns described, remember that we all have self-defeating behaviors. The patterns in this book are extremely common. Many of us, including me, have been there, done that, got the T-shirt when it comes to these issues. Shame and self-criticism are counterproductive to moving forward and are not warranted. Also keep in mind that a book like this will attract readers who lean toward perfectionism and taking excessive responsibility. You may feel as if you are making a complete mess of managing your life, happiness, and relationships. If you think that, pay attention to what you're doing right as well as what you're doing wrong. There's a saying from the mindfulness tradition that goes, "If you're breathing, there's more right with you than there is wrong with you." If you found your way to this book, you clearly have good problem-solving instincts and the capacity to execute a strategy for helping yourself. Paying attention to only what you perceive you're doing wrong is itself a self-sabotaging pattern. How so? It strips you of the confidence and sense of self-command you need to implement change. When people intellectually understand cognitive behavioral skills but struggle to feel and act better, it's often lack of self-compassion and the ongoing presence of shame and self-criticism that are holding them back.[2]

In addition, if, as you read, you find that you have difficulty prioritizing which patterns to target, there's a good chance it's because you're a self-critical perfectionist. When you have extremely high standards for yourself, small imperfections, errors, and inefficiencies can feel just as intolerable as large ones. The perfectionist is as likely to unload a barrage of self-criticism in response to the small missteps as to the large ones. Self-critical perfectionists ruminate over small mistakes, which causes the pain to linger well past the event and turns molehills into mountains. Perfectionists often don't see themselves as self-critical, even though everyone else does. Because they expect themselves to be flawless, they see the self-criticism as justified and don't recognize how severe it is. I'll help you address this issue as we proceed together.

SELF-SABOTAGE HACK

If you're unsure if you're being too hard on yourself, try asking yourself, if a boss were speaking to me or treating me as I'm currently treating myself, would I be upset and angry about that and think they were unfair or overly harsh? If the answer is yes, you know it's time to treat yourself a little more kindly!

Troubleshooting tips: If anything you read here leaves you feeling worse about yourself, you might be (1) reacting to the material with self-criticism, (2) setting unrealistically high expectations for yourself, (3) over-complicating potential solutions, or (4) a combination of these. Notice if any of this happens. Remind yourself that these reactions are part of the trap of self-sabotage. Frustration and shame bog you down and stop you from climbing out of your patterns.

Experiment

Identify the area of your life in which self-sabotage is having the greatest impact for you—for example, eating, organization, or the ways you relate to others. Try asking yourself, What do I already do right in that area? For example, for the domain of healthy eating, you could list that you take lunch to work, eat oatmeal for breakfast every morning, don't tend to eat after dinner, and don't buy a lot of takeout.

When you identify what you're doing right, you can see you're not starting from zero. You have a base of skills and good habits you can build on. If you have a sense of currently being at zero, making changes will feel unnecessarily daunting.

Believe in Your Capacity to Find Solutions to Your Self-Defeating Habits

If, as you move through the rest of these chapters, you feel like there is a lot to take in, it's because there is. While the book has dozens of simple, actionable tips, I've also included a lot of nuance and depth to help you thoroughly understand the sometimes intricate psychology behind self-sabotage. Human nature is complex. You may need to reread sections a few times to get your head around certain concepts or to reconcile advice that on the surface seems to contradict other advice. Low tolerance for ambiguity and shades of gray are aspects of many of the self-sabotaging patterns that hold people back in life.[3] Coping with any uncertainty you feel as you read, without abandoning the change process, is an important component of freeing yourself from the burden of self-sabotage.

On the bright side, the more you practice looking for solutions to your self-defeating patterns and implementing them, the better you'll get at it. Everyone's first steps will be finding solutions or partial solutions to just a few problems. Even when you're starting out, you'll get the following benefits from practicing the strategies in *The Healthy Mind Toolkit*:

- With practice, you'll become better at noticing your self-defeating habits. Instead of just coping with the consequences, you'll start to look out for how to prevent the patterns occurring in the first place.
- You'll start to react less passively to your patterns and will remember to ask yourself, "What strategy could I apply here?"
- Your confidence in your capacity to find creative solutions will grow.
- The more you practice using strategies, the better you'll get at knowing which options you've realistically got the energy to implement. You'll also start to see ways to make your strategies simpler and easier.
- Some solutions can be reused for different situations and problems, either in a modified form or as is. For example, perspective taking (by which you mentally put yourself in someone else's shoes to understand their thoughts and feelings) is a skill that's useful at home for understanding your partner and at work for understanding your customers. If you practice this skill in one life domain, you'll automatically become better at doing it in the other areas (skills tend to automatically transfer from one life domain to others more easily than insights).
- Your identity will shift. You will go from seeing yourself as someone who has poor or average skills for dealing with self-sabotage, to someone who is on their way to being an expert.

Preparing for Self-Experiments

Throughout the book, I offer short experiments similar to the two I've already included in this chapter. Some are thought experiments that involve only writing down your thoughts, but others also involve taking action. *You don't need to try every experiment.* Focus on what seems most relevant to you and fits with your current priorities. A good approach is to treat the book as a reference guide. You don't need to master everything—only what's most important to you right now. You can dip back into the book when you want solutions for a particular problem, whether that's in a few months or in a few years.

While you're reading, you'll need a place to write your answers to the thought experiments and to record any other take-home messages you want to remember. Use anything that works for you, whether that's a physical notebook, a Google Doc, the notes app on your phone, or you could write your answers in emails to yourself (*tip*: use a consistent subject line so you can find those emails later).

Why is it important to take active notes like this? Writing down your responses to thought experiments will often generate different light-bulb moments compared to if you only think about the experiments, so that's why I strongly recommend you record your thoughts in written form for maximum benefit. If you're not the writing type, you can always do an alternative, like talking through the thought experiment with a friend. If you prefer to work visually, you can draw your answers using pictures, little graphs, or flowcharts. You can also mix and match your approach, depending on what you feel like, what you have time for, and whatever seems most useful for a particular experiment.

Sometimes thought experiments trigger a sense of being put on the spot or tested. There's no test, folks. If you feel anxious or frozen in re-action to the idea of doing experiments, know that doing even the tiniest amount of thinking about the question at hand can help you get unfrozen. If you prefer, you can keep reading until you come across an experiment that feels manageable to you. Use some Post-it flags (or something similar) to mark the places where you read something particularly useful to you or experiments you want to try later.

As a general principle, answer the thought experiments according to whatever your first instinct is, without overthinking. There are lots of ways of approaching them. Pick a way. It doesn't have to be the absolute best approach. Adapt and simplify any of the thought experiments as you see fit, unless noted. If I suggest coming up with three examples and you'd prefer to write only one to make the experiment more manageable with the energy you have, do that. You're in charge! And you're an adult with lots of competing priorities and responsibilities.

Why It's Important to Test the Ideas from This Book in Your Own Life

Psychology became a science, in the way people tend to think of a science today, only in the 1890s. Subfields, like relationships psychology, are much, much younger still. For instance, the study of love exploded only in the late 1980s, and the study of other types of positive emotions and of concepts like happiness and meaning in life didn't begin in earnest until the 1990s. At this point, we have many thousands of scientific studies on a wide variety of aspects of human nature, but there are still huge gaps in the research literature.

In addition, research studies tend to be best at describing the "average" participant (typically college students). There is a lot we don't know about what applies when, to whom, and what the exceptions are. It's very common for conclusions and advice to get revised (and sometimes even reversed) as new data emerge (as happens in many fields, including in medicine and the physical health sciences). Therefore, use what you read here as a starting point for your own investigations into yourself. Combine what you learn from reading with what you learn from testing the principles discussed in your own life.

A final note is that I've included links to any resources I've mentioned in the book at http://healthymindtoolkit.com/resources. If anything I've referenced has been moved or removed, I'll try to provide new links or alternatives on that web page. You can also check out the website for bonus content related to the book.

THE NERD'S GUIDE TO SELF-EXPERIMENTS

If you want a scientifically rigorous way to understand the effectiveness of your behavioral changes, you can use what's known as an ABAB experiment. Let's consider an example in which you want to see if taking a lunchtime walk helps you feel happier and regulate your other behavior better. In this experiment type, you'd start by recording a baseline for whatever outcome variables you're interested in, without doing anything else differently. This baseline is the first *A* in ABAB. Each day for a week, you might record the time you go to bed, or do a 1–7 self-rating of your mood as you're leaving work for the day (1 = extremely unhappy; 7 = extremely happy). Ideally, measure several different outcome variables as part of the same experiment.

You would then introduce whatever intervention you wanted to try. For example, going for a thirty-minute walk at lunchtime. That's your first *B*. You would continue to record your outcome variable each day (your mood at the end of the day and your bedtime). After a week of going for a walk at lunchtime every day, you'd go back to your *A* condition of not going for a walk, and continue your recordings. In the fourth week, you'd reintroduce your intervention (your walk) and do your last week of ratings, completing your final

B step. If you observe that you go to bed earlier or feel better in both *B* weeks, compared to both *A* weeks, you'll know you're more likely to have observed a real effect. You're not blind to your own hypotheses so any outcome could still be a placebo effect. However, using an ABAB design helps you know that differences you observe aren't due to unrelated factors, like your work being less (or more) busy from one week to the next. You don't have to use this format, but if you're a measurement geek, this is an option.

Are You Ready to Get Started?

If you'd like a checklist to determine whether you're done with this chapter and are ready to move on, you can use this one. If you answer yes to all three questions, you're ready to proceed.

❏ Did you set a goal for what you want to achieve from using this book? Did you double-check that your goal is reasonable for the time and energy you have available?

❏ Have you set yourself up with either a physical or electronic notepad for recording your thoughts as you read? Do you have a highlighter and some Post-it flags for marking points you want to be able to easily refer back to?

❏ Have you identified what you most want to remember from this chapter? If you didn't already, pick 1–3 take-home messages now.

CHAPTER 2

· · · · · · · · · · · · · · · · · · ·

Diagnosing Your
Self-Sabotaging Patterns

At the beginning of chapter 1, I gave examples of self-defeating patterns that seem like opposites but, as I mentioned, are really two sides of the same coin. Both extremes are self-defeating, and these paired patterns have especially wide-ranging implications across different life domains. In this chapter, we look more at these.

Experiment

Simple option: Flip back to the table of paired statements on pages 5–7. Imagine a four- to five-inch line running from each sabotaging pattern to its opposite pair. Where would you fall on that line? You can use the template you'll find at http://healthymindtoolkit.com/resources to mark where your behavior sits.

More detailed option: Given that people are complex, you may not be able to put just one mark per line to fully encapsulate all your behavior. Therefore, another option is to put two marks per line. Label one of the marks with an *M* to indicate where *most* of your behavior falls, and the other *S* for *sometimes*. Use the printable template from the resources webpage to do this.

What Makes Both Extremes Self-Defeating?

On the following pages I've unpacked seven example pairs in detail to illustrate why each extreme is self-sabotaging. You may want to scan ahead to see which pairs I've included and skip to whichever you're most interested in first. Because my descriptions are generalizations, I may mention a point that doesn't apply to you or you may think of points that are personally relevant that I haven't covered.

Given that your problem will typically be more with one half of the pair than the other, you might be asking yourself, Why do I need to understand both ends of the spectrum? Often what drives people to behave in an extreme way is fear that, if they don't, they'll end up going too far in the other direction. For example, you overwork because you think that, if you don't, you'll somehow become someone who underworks. Or you're very suspicious of others because you fear that you'll be too trusting, naive, or gullible if you don't keep your BS radar set to high alert. Articulating the problems associated with behavior that's opposite of your dominant pattern will help you face those fears.

When we fear something, we usually attempt to avoid thinking about it.[1] Consequently, you might not recognize how unlikely it is you'd end up consistently doing the opposite of what you do now. It's unlikely that a pessimist will suddenly become excessively optimistic or that a workaholic will become a slacker after easing up a bit. In fact, when we temporarily flip to the other extreme in certain circumstances, it's usually our extreme behavior that's driving that flipping. For example, someone who overworks during the workweek may be so tired when they take a day off, all they do is veg out.

Another reason for understanding both your style and its opposite is to better understand other people. As you read, if you don't relate to a particular pattern personally, ask yourself if understanding that pattern could help you comprehend the behavior of someone in your life—for example, a family member, close co-worker, friend, or boss.

Let's start by investigating the consequences of too much chaos versus too much routine.

PROBLEMS CAUSED BY NOT ENOUGH ROUTINE

You expend too much energy making frequent decisions. If you had more routine you wouldn't spend as much energy and time thinking about when, where, or how to do things. Without routines, you end up being inefficient in the way you go about your regular activities. It's harder to optimize your behavior when you're inconsistent. Chaos makes it easier to repeatedly avoid essential tasks because it's easier to ignore an action if you don't have a set time and place for it.

PROBLEMS CAUSED BY TOO MUCH ROUTINE

Life gets monotonous. Days blur into the next. Activities you do often lose their luster—for example, a high-end coffee every day isn't as special as having one once in a while.[2] You don't get to enjoy the pleasure of spontaneity. If you're always following the same routine, you're less likely to have the types of novel or random experiences that can enhance your joy and creativity, such as bumping into new people, or encountering cues in the environment that make you think about something in a new way. If you experience yourself in only a limited range of circumstances, you may see your personality, talents, and capabilities more narrowly than they really are. You miss out on the fact it can be more enjoyable and/or more productive to do certain activities when you're in the mood for them rather than on a set schedule.

PROBLEMS CAUSED BY GIVING UP TOO SOON

You experience unnecessary instances of failure and the accompanying unpleasant emotions. You achieve less than you're capable of and therefore miss out on comforts that come from achievement, such as higher income or being in work roles that have more autonomy. You don't get an accurate picture of whether your ideas are good because you don't fully test them. You don't gain experience and confidence in your ability to work through problems. You may mislabel yourself as stupid or a loser. You don't develop your grit and therefore, over time, it becomes harder to persist when you experience challenges. This is the same principle as how, when you don't exercise, it becomes progressively harder to do so because you become more and more unfit. When you give up quickly, other people may view you as flaky and lacking self-discipline and become annoyed with you. If you sense that others lack confidence in you, it will erode your confidence in yourself.

PROBLEMS CAUSED BY PERSISTING TOO MUCH

People who overpersist tend to keep hammering away at problems using their dominant strategies, even if those options are ineffective or inefficient in their current circumstances. You avoid taking breaks. When you're chronically exhausted, it's harder to think and behave flexibly. You become even less likely to step back, get a broad perspective on what you're doing, and become more strategic. If overpersisting is intermittently rewarded (that is, sometimes results in success) then persisting may become compulsive. You may find yourself committing the *sunk costs error* of evaluating whether you should continue with a behavior based on how many resources (time, effort, and/or money) you've already sunk into it. For example, if you've already waited on hold for ten minutes, you keep waiting when you really need to be getting on to another task. If you develop a self-identity as someone who never gives up, it becomes difficult to selectively choose when to bail out. Other people may view you as dogmatic and inflexible. You may assign your personal standards for persistence to other people and unreasonably think that they should persist to the same extent you do. This can cause problems in your close relationships and/or result in your being an ineffective and disliked leader.

PROBLEMS CAUSED BY BEING TOO OPTIMISTIC

You may not be self-protective enough. Because you don't think bad things will happen to you, you don't take proper precautions. You may be too trusting of others. Excessive optimism can generate stress. For example, if you experience unexpected costs and then find it difficult to pay your mortgage. Setbacks may be more difficult to cope with when you don't have a plan B: You plan an outdoor wedding, it rains, and you don't have a backup plan. Optimistic people may spread themselves too thin because they take on too many activities. Over optimism can result in annoying and inconveniencing others. For example, if you plan to be exactly on time and assume everything will go right (no delays or hiccups), the reality might be that you're frequently late. Risk taking that's driven by overoptimism (like not wearing sunblock or not having health insurance) may be anxiety provoking for your loved ones as well as detrimental to you.

PROBLEMS CAUSED BY BEING TOO PESSIMISTIC

You hold back from attempting to achieve your goals because you expect you won't succeed. Due to your pessimism, you react negatively to ideas other people have, which they may find irritating and demoralizing. You close yourself off from potential enjoyment—for example, you expect yourself not to enjoy a conference, so you choose not to go. You may perceive yourself as having lots of ideas but that none of them pan out, when it's not that you didn't succeed but rather that you didn't actually try your ideas. Over time, this pattern reinforces your pessimism and the notion that most ideas don't bear fruit. Because you foresee so many problems, you get overwhelmed and don't differentiate between important and unimportant problems. You exhaust yourself planning for problems that may never eventuate. You don't ask for help because you assume other people either won't want to help you or, if they do try, won't be useful to you.

PROBLEMS CAUSED BY UNDERTHINKING DECISIONS (BEING TOO IMPULSIVE)

The underthinker endures the consequences of bad decisions made impulsively. If you think of yourself as an unskilled decision maker, you may become even more impulsive because you have no faith in your reasoning abilities and just want to get decision making over and done with. You may lose the support and trust of other people who are impacted by your poorly thought out decisions.

PROBLEMS CAUSED BY OVERTHINKING DECISIONS

When people habitually overthink, making decisions can feel very stressful or even incapacitating—for example, you feel physically frozen. Overthinking often results in becoming more confused and can waste a lot of time and energy. By avoiding action, you lose the opportunity to learn from experience. For example, you never learn that making a less-than-perfect decision may be better overall compared to the excessive time and energy involved in making a slightly better choice. You don't give yourself a chance to learn, experientially, that if you do find yourself feeling regret, it's generally a less intense and more tolerable feeling than you anticipated. The harder you work to avoid making any mistakes in your decisions, the more intolerable it feels when mistakes are invariably made. You may lose out on time-limited opportunities because of your delays, such as if an item sells out while you're debating whether to purchase it. You may frustrate and infuriate others, as when a household item breaks but you can't decide what replacement to get.

PROBLEMS CAUSED BY BEING TOO FOCUSED ON YOUR CURRENT WANTS

The consequences of being too focused on what you want right now are obvious. If you always give in to your current wants at the expense of long-term goals, overall you'll end up having less of the things you want compared to someone who is prepared to wait to experience more benefits later. You may frequently mispredict what will make you happy and fall victim to the *liking versus wanting bias* (see chapter 13 for more about this bias).

PROBLEMS CAUSED BY DELAYING GRATIFICATION TOO MUCH

If you're overfocused on delayed gratification you end up out of touch with what actually gives you pleasure. For example, you save up the money to do a yearlong international trip without doing smaller trips first, only to find out you don't enjoy international travel as much as you expected. You may find it hard to break the habit of delaying gratification when you reach the point of wanting to indulge. You may also lack skills in spending money optimally. For example, you're saving to one day build your dream home but you don't spend any money improving your current home. When you come to build your dream house, you don't have any experience with planning, decorating, or working with contractors. Other people may find your extreme future focus irritating— for example, when one spouse wants to spend money now and the other doesn't. Being very future focused in a few areas of life but not in other domains can lead to a lack of balance, as does an overworker who sacrifices their health.

PROBLEMS CAUSED BY NOT TAKING ENOUGH RESPONSIBILITY AND BLAMING OTHERS

When you blame others for your behavior, it's often still going to be you who ends up suffering the consequences. For example, if you blame your spouse for why you don't eat healthfully, it's still you who ends up overweight. Likewise, if you blame your partner for why you don't have much closeness and pleasure in your relationship, it's still you who misses out on that. Blaming others is a way of giving yourself permission to avoid taking action. Blaming others and using justifications go hand in hand. For example, you tell yourself that the reason you don't help out more at home is because your spouse has high standards and always criticizes you. Avoidance of responsibility may result in antagonism and resentment in your relationships. You'll be less likely to genuinely apologize after you've done something wrong, which can hold up the process of getting forgiven for whatever mistake you've made. This pattern of behavior may make you unappealing as someone to work or live with. When you blame others, you don't self-reflect on your own behavior and therefore lose the opportunity to address what might be easily fixable self-sabotaging habits.

PROBLEMS CAUSED BY TAKING TOO MUCH RESPONSIBILITY

Taking excessive responsibility creates anxiety and is even implicated in anxiety disorders.[3] Feeling responsible for anything and everything can result in getting overwhelmed and not prioritizing what's really important. Getting caught up in small issues can give you an excuse to avoid more major decisions. Paradoxically, you may avoid roles that involve responsibility (such as leadership positions) because responsibility feels so burdensome. Feeling responsible for helping other people avoid bad decisions may result in your repeatedly nagging them. What's more, people may get lazy if you do everything for them and are constantly there to help and remind them. For example, if you provide tech support for family members whenever they need it, they may never learn any tech skills themselves. If you eventually get fed up with always helping and reminding them, you may find they're legitimately unable to help themselves because they've developed no skills of their own.

PROBLEMS CAUSED BY THINKING TOO BIG

If you think too big, other people may be freaked out by the size of your plans and risk taking. For example, you want to convince your spouse to purchase an investment property to rent out. You're a big thinker so you start talking about buying ten investment properties and building an empire. In this scenario, your spouse may be less likely to go along with your plans than if you'd proposed something smaller to start. Without buy-in from others, you're potentially less likely to realize your plans. People (including you) may start to view you as someone who has a lot of ideas but doesn't deliver. If you think big, you can sometimes get caught up in fantasizing about your success, which, paradoxically, may demotivate you when it comes to the step-by-step actions you need to take now. The reality of the work to be done may seem boring compared to your fantasies of large-scale success, so you lose motivation.[4] If you think too big and attempt to run before you can walk, you may reduce your future opportunities. For example, if you incur bankruptcy or damage your credit.

PROBLEMS CAUSED BY THINKING TOO SMALL

If you defensively set small goals (that is, you aim small to avoid triggering anxiety about whether you can reach larger targets), you might fail to achieve even the small goals because you don't employ the strategies that people who aim bigger use. For example, you're nervous to employ anyone. Therefore, you set yourself up in business as a one-man band, but you don't get ahead because you're trying to do everything yourself. There's an opportunity cost to thinking conservatively. When you're caught up in chasing small wins, you may overlook the bigger picture. Busying yourself with small projects can distract you from larger opportunities. Over time, you may end up believing you think small because you're capable of achieving only at that level, rather than recognizing that you've set your sights low out of anxiety and habit. If you think too small, you may not realize it's objectively riskier than thinking bigger. For example, you have an eBay business. You focus on sourcing items to sell that will net you a 5-to-10-percent profit. That's potentially more risky (due to unforeseen costs or market changes) than pursuing strategies that will earn a 30-to-40-percent profit, even if sourcing profitable products seems harder in the beginning. If you think too small, other people may not find your moderate plans motivating or interesting; therefore, you may struggle to get buy-in from others (just as the person who thinks too big does).

Experiment

Now it's your turn. By unpacking just one of your self-sabotaging patterns in detail, as I've done in the examples, you'll learn to see when making nonextreme choices could benefit you and how you can minimize the downsides of your dominant style. If I've already dissected the pattern that's of most interest to you, try making a simple flowchart to visually depict how the pattern manifests for you. Put the elements in the flowchart that are most relevant to you. You don't need to include everything I have. If I haven't unpacked the pattern you'd like to focus on, do it for yourself, using the examples as a guide. *Tip*: To get breadth in your analysis, think about the impact of the pattern in various life domains. For example, how does the pattern affect your work, home life, and friendships? It's important to understand both the personal and the interpersonal consequences of your thinking/behavioral style.

Now What? Finding the Middle Path

Experiment

For whatever pattern you picked for the last experiment, identify one very specific situation in your life in which it is currently causing a problem for you. First, articulate your pattern. For example, let's say you're someone who feels easily bored by routine. You run to the supermarket almost every day because you never plan out more than one day's meals in advance. You keep little extra food at home. You value flexibility so highly you don't want to commit to buying items you might not feel like later. However, you've recognized these habits are getting time-consuming, are expensive, and aren't great for your health. In particular, you're eating lots of prepared meals because whenever you feel like cooking from scratch you don't have the ingredients, and it's too time and energy sapping to shop and then cook the same evening.

Next, ask yourself two additional questions:

How would someone who is the opposite of me think and act in this situation?

How would someone who is in the middle of the two extremes think and act?

Articulating what someone at the opposite extreme would do makes it quick and easy to identify what the middle path is. For the food shopping example, the person who has too much routine may plan out all their meals in advance, shop for the same items every month, and eat the same meals week in, week out.

How would a middle ground person approach this? How would he think and behave? Let's say Mr. Middle Ground works late on Mondays and Tuesdays, so he comes home and either makes a quick omelet for dinner or eats a fairly healthful meal he microwaves out of the freezer. On Wednesdays he usually gets home early, so he cooks enough to eat leftovers the next night. His Friday-night ritual is buying his favorite takeout. On the weekend he shops for the week, and he keeps his weekend meals flexible. This balance works well for him. He doesn't always feel like sticking to his routines, but he values how much his patterns streamline his life.

Use this framework to identify potential middle paths for situations in which you'd normally swing toward a self-defeating extreme. At first you may find it easier to do this retrospectively. You might look back on a situation after it's occurred and think about how you could behave differently in a similar scenario in the future. With practice, you'll start to be able to use the framework in real time.

IMPORTANT!

Is the middle path always the best option? Not necessarily. For example, thinking very big, being very persistent, or overworking can be the most fruitful thing to do in certain circumstances. By thinking through the options for how you could behave, you gain the flexibility to choose a path based on your assessment of a specific situation rather than just acting in a certain way out of habit or doing what's most psychologically comfortable for you. Choose whatever has the best combination of high upside and low downside in that particular circumstance. The take-home message is to choose the optimal thinking and behavior style for the specific situation you're in, after considering the personal and interpersonal (relationship) implications and short- and long-term consequences. In some cases, this may even involve going to the other extreme from how you'd typically behave, if you can see an enormous potential upside of doing that. I'll outline some of the potential benefits of extreme thinking and behavior in the next section.

Understanding the Strengths of Your Nature

The more extreme a trait is, the more likely it has both positive and negative consequences for you.[5] Understanding that your tendencies have useful upsides as well as downsides will help you develop more flexibility to go with your dominant nature when it makes sense to do so but to shift your approach when it doesn't.

There is very little that humans do that has no positives associated with it. That simply wouldn't make sense from an evolutionary standpoint. Different thinking and behavioral styles suit different circumstances, and all kinds of minds can contribute to groups performing optimally (whether families, work teams, or governments). Even traits like narcissism have a demonstrated upside—for example, narcissists' disdain for rules can produce creative solutions that people with more deference to rules don't generate.[6]

When you recognize the strengths of your dominant style, this can help dissolve any defensiveness you feel toward addressing situations in which it flips over into being suboptimal. Dissolving defensiveness and shame is almost certainly going to help you make the smartest situation-specific choices.

Let's look at some examples of how extreme tendencies can be helpful.

- Thinking very big can help you see past conventional assumptions that may be limiting you.[7] You may also have less competition if you think way bigger than your competitors. And going big can sometimes, paradoxically, be less risky than thinking smaller—for example, if your risk is more diversified, such as you buy ten properties of different types in different geographic markets rather than a single property.

- If you tend to nitpick and get excessively focused on small details, there is clearly an upside to that. It might help you succeed in some aspects of your career, for instance, if you're a wedding planner. If you tend to be negative and disagreeable, that's potentially beneficial when others might blindly go along with problematic ideas.

- In my first book, *The Anxiety Toolkit*, I wrote about the benefits of having a style of thinking known as *defensive pessimism*. This style is characterized by hoping for the best but anticipating and preparing for problems. There are many upsides to care and caution, before they start spilling over into paralysis. In fact, a combination of hope and moderate anxiety may be the most optimal thinking style in many situations. People who are hopeful but who are also little bit anxious straddle the chasm between optimism (everything will be fine) and pessimism (nothing will be fine). They combine the benefits of hope (which include tolerance of ambiguity, willingness to act, and humility) with the benefits of caution.[8]

- Being willing to break rules can lead to succeeding where others who have tried to work within the rules have failed.
- Impulsiveness frees you from overthinking and can result in a mixture of good and bad decision making. You may have talked yourself out of a beneficial decision if you'd thought more.
- Being very persistent will often result in wearing other people down to the point they give in to what you want. This may not have major social costs if you don't need to maintain an ongoing relationship with those people.

The Silver Lining Strategy

Another way extreme tendencies can benefit people lies in the fact that our traits tend to shape our skills. When your traits result in having a weakness, you may end up developing a strength to compensate. There's research showing that seeing a silver lining to your "negative" attributes increases effort and heightens performance sometimes in unexpectedly beneficial ways.[9] For example, I'm a sensitive introvert and feel a lot of social obligation when I have friends who live in the same city as I do. Consequently, I almost prefer having friends who live other places and whom I see in person once, or a few times, a year when I'm traveling. As a result, I've become very good at keeping in touch with people I don't see much, and I'm still able to form deep friendships with them.

As a flowchart, this pattern looks like the following:

My weakness: Feeling easily overwhelmed by social obligations.

▼

My preference: Having friends who live in various parts
of the country/world.

▼

My strength: Keeping in touch with people
whom I don't see in person often.

Here's another example of this strategy. A friend of mine recently shared a story about how her (unfounded) lack of confidence in her work skills has resulted in her becoming very good at asking questions at work-related education meetings. Even though she is socially anxious, her anxiety about not knowing the answer to her question is stronger than her anxiety about putting her hand up. She regularly gets feedback from others about how good her questions are and how others were wondering the same thing but felt too inhibited to ask.

Her version of the flowchart is as follows:

Her weakness: Lacking confidence about her work skills.

▼

Her preference: Double-checking and clarifying her
understanding of concepts.

▼

Her strength: Asking questions at education meetings.

If your default style leans toward being extreme and you recognize it has some costs for you, seeing the strengths of your nature will help you avoid thinking of yourself as crazy or weird or getting bogged down due to lack of confidence. Indulging your natural tendencies will sometimes have an acceptable cost to benefit ratio, and sometimes it won't. When it doesn't, you have other options, which you can identify using the *middle path technique.*

Experiment

Try creating your own version of the flowchart.

Another Way to Identify Self-Defeating Patterns You Potentially Overlook

People sometimes have a blind spot for self-defeating patterns when a skill or trait is an overall strength for them. For example, you see yourself as having great self-control but your self-control is poor when it comes to inhibiting your urge to snap at your partner when you're feeling hurt. Or you're generally very good at managing your money, or eating healthfully, but not in certain small pockets of relative weakness.

What can be satisfying (and even enjoyable) about tackling patterns of this type is that, by definition, these self-defeating habits are in areas in which you feel generally confident and competent.

Experiment

To identify problems that fit this description, try asking yourself the following questions in this order:

What strengths are core parts of your self-identity? (What you identify as your strengths can be as broad or specific as you like. You could pick a very broad strength, like self-control, or be more specific, like you excel at delegating/outsourcing or prioritizing.)

Where do you have pockets of weakness within these strengths?

What are the personality traits, well-established good habits, or strategies that help create your general area of strength?

How could you use those traits and strategies to overcome your pocket of weakness? For now, brainstorm one specific way.

Here's a (hypothetical) example fleshed out, so you can see how to go about this process.

Questions	Answers
What is one of my core strengths?	Self-control.
What is an area of weakness within that strength?	Nitpicking my spouse when it doesn't make logical sense to do so.
What are the personality traits, cognitive abilities, and/or good habits or strategies that create my general area of strength?	My cognitive abilities let me pause, step back, and see the big picture. My emotion skills allow me to calm myself down in heated moments.
How I could use these traits, abilities, or habits/strategies, to overcome my relative weakness?	I could better consider the long-term impact of nitpicking and choose my battles more judiciously.

Moving On

Try answering the following questions before moving on to the next chapter.

❑ For the pattern you chose to unpack for the extremes versus middle path experiment, do you have any upcoming situations that will provide an opportunity to try out the middle path?

❏ If you were to come back and focus on some of the other patterns later, what would be on your "maybe later" list? Identify up to three additional patterns.

❏ What are the 1–3 points that most resonated with you in this chapter?

CHAPTER 3

The Reasons People Stay Stuck in Self-Sabotaging Habits

Why Do People Get Caught in Self-Defeating Cycles?

The following sections provide an explanation of four core reasons self-defeating habits persist. This list is not exhaustive because we'll cover this topic throughout the book, but it's a good start.

A. You Lack Accurate Insight into Your Patterns

Here's an example of self-sabotage caused by an insight problem. One of my personal self-defeating behaviors is task switching. I flit around from one half-finished job to another, rather than doing activities in a logical order and completing each one before moving on to the next. This problem existed for far too long before I realized my underlying issue isn't actually being unable to stick with and complete one task at a time. Rather it's that I don't take frequent enough breaks. Task switching is what I do when I'm tired and start to lose concentration. Eventually I noticed I rarely abandon partly finished work in the first hour after starting; it happens only when I'm becoming exhausted from concentrating too long without giving my brain a quick rest. If I were to target the problem of task switching itself, I'd be attempting to solve the wrong issue. Any solution I came up with for reducing task switching would likely require using willpower at exactly the time my willpower is in short supply, and the resulting failure would perpetuate my pattern of self-sabotage. What I in fact need to do is recognize that the urge to change tasks is a sign that I need a break and so should take one. Even though this seems incredibly simple, in truth, it took a while to understand the real dynamics of the problem, even for me.

B. You Have Poor Problem Orientation

In essence, someone who has poor problem orientation doesn't respond to problems by following a streamlined process of identifying the problem, generating potential solutions, picking one, and deploying it. People who worry a lot often have poor problem orientation.[1] You know you have this issue if you find yourself letting significant problems drag on, not because they're unsolvable but because you don't take the time to go through a simple problem-solving process to choose the best available solution. The common reasons this happens include the following:

You're habitually avoidant.

You're overwhelmed by many anxieties, so you don't pick out the solvable problems. You don't distinguish between current challenges that actually need solutions and the types of worries that are mainly outside your control (such as how other people will think and behave) or situations in which you're already employing the right solutions (for example, to stay in good health you eat pretty well, stay physically active, get a flu shot every year, and keep up to date with all your regular medical screenings). When you don't mentally differentiate between worries that need solutions and those that don't, you don't immediately jump to fixing the easily solvable issues and end up ruminating about problems that aren't within your control to resolve or those for which you're already doing everything you can or need to do.

You don't have confidence in your capacity to problem solve. You've depleted your self-confidence through self-criticism.

You're a perfectionistic ruminator who tends to overthink problems and overcomplicate solutions. You're therefore even more anxious about approaching problem solving because it seems so complex and fraught.

Note that throughout the book I use a broad definition of *problem*. Your problem could be that you want to move to Hawaii and don't know how to start figuring out how you'll do that. *Problem solving*, as I'm using the term, isn't just about dealing with frustrations, it's also about going after what you want.

C. Your Self-Sabotaging Behavior Is Getting Intermittently Reinforced

Intermittent reinforcement is when a behavior sometimes results in a payoff and sometimes doesn't. Let's look at three classic examples to illustrate the concept.

Gambling.

You constantly nag your spouse, and it occasionally results in your spouse doing what you want.

You worry a lot. Even if most of the time your worry ends up being pointless, occasionally it helps you avoid a problem.

When a behavior gets intermittently reinforced, even very infrequent payoffs can keep you deeply hooked into that behavior. Your behavior might have a hugely negative overall impact on your life and relationships, but intermittent reinforcement pulls you into continuing it. One reason intermittent reinforcement can be such a problem is that when a behavior is sometimes rewarded, we tend to escalate that behavior whenever we don't get a payoff. For example, if nagging doesn't succeed at first, you nag more or louder. Therefore, not only do intermittently reinforced behaviors continue but they also tend to intensify over time.

D. Staying Stuck Is More Comfortable Than Getting Unstuck

Imagine you were to take a perfectionistic approach to this book. As you read, you criticize yourself for how much self-sabotage you do. However, as someone who wants to eliminate all self-sabotage, you avoid prioritizing which of your self-defeating patterns are the most important to target. And instead of actually trying out some suggested strategies, you ruminate about all the mistakes you've made in the past and continue to make.

Ruminating feels miserable. However, it has a hidden payoff. Your comfort zone has become avoiding and ruminating, rather than taking action. By criticizing yourself so much that you don't believe in your capacity to self-experiment, you give yourself an excuse to get out of doing it. Even though criticism, rumination, and avoidance feel bad, they're still more comfortable than attempting experiments and going beyond your comfort zone. They're frenemies. The devil you know is less scary than trying something new because it doesn't involve any large emotional swings. You can stay on your perch looking out for things that could go wrong, rather than venturing out into the unknown.[2]

Even if you're not prone to rumination or worry, choosing to go beyond your comfort zone takes mental and emotional energy. If you move through life feeling exhausted, at critical decision points you likely won't have the willpower available to think about and choose the less psychologically comfortable but more beneficial option. Let's run through another example. Take someone who identifies that they have a self-sabotaging pattern of failing to delegate. They know it's a problem but nothing changes. Their problem is with *doing what they know* rather than *knowing what to do*. Why don't they act on their insight?

If a person keeps up a behavior repeatedly, we can assume that even if the way they're doing things is hard, it must not be as hard for them as the alternatives. For example, for someone who could delegate but doesn't, doing all the work themselves must not be as hard as (1) explaining the task to someone else and/or (2) feeling anxiety about whether the person is going to do the task to their standards and/or (3) tolerating the feeling of not being indispensable. At least initially, delegating feels more psychologically challenging than doing everything themselves. When we're mentally exhausted, we tend to do whatever is the least challenging.

SELF-SABOTAGE HACK

If you find yourself repeating a pattern of behavior that doesn't seem useful, instead of criticizing yourself, ask yourself, "By doing what I'm doing, am I giving myself permission to opt out of taking an action that I would find more psychologically challenging?"

Experiment

Now that you've read about the four mechanisms that snare people in self-defeating habits, rank them according to how much each applies to you, 1 = most relevant to me; 4 = least relevant to me. You'll end up with a list that looks something like 1 = D, 2 = B, 3 = C, and 4 = A.

Did you gain something from learning about these mechanisms? If yes, what? What light bulbs went off for you? What could you relate to? Are your issues mostly about knowing what to do or doing what you know?

Collect Easy Wins

Let's cover another thinking bias involved in why, even when people have great ideas for how to overcome self-sabotage, they may not implement their insights. Evolutionary processes have equipped us with extremely useful capacities to take mental shortcuts. However, sometimes those shortcuts lead to thinking errors. An example of this is that our brains typically equate how difficult it is to achieve something with how valuable it is. The harder we work at something, the more valuable we perceive it to be. Your brain may devalue the easy wins you could achieve in overcoming self-sabotage.

Perfectionists are particularly prone to being dismissive of incremental changes or improvements. Say that putting your ice cream at the back of your freezer results in eating ice cream 20 percent less often compared to keeping it in the front, where you see it every time you open the door. This is a very small behavioral change that requires no real effort or sacrifice. However, perfectionists are not very likely to see this type of solution as valuable. They want to feel 100 percent in control of how much ice cream they eat and when. Because eating 20 percent less ice cream is an incremental gain that improves the problem but may not solve it completely, perfectionists devalue this solution. They may be dismissive of it and are less likely to bother implementing it, which results in less success in managing their ice cream consumption overall. They also miss an easy opportunity to build their problem-solving skills and confidence.

Even problems that are very impactful and are difficult to change overall will often have aspects that are easy to change—and those small behavior modifications are worth it! The problem of overeating is, in general, a complex, hard-to-change problem. However, as illustrated by the ice cream example, there are some simple, behavioral easy wins that take virtually no willpower or concentration to implement. Don't underestimate the value of incremental changes. Even 10 percent changes in patterns can have a huge impact, and in some cases, they can resolve the problem entirely or at least greatly lessen its negative impact.

Examples:

If your weight is steadily creeping up a little bit each year, reducing your intake by 10 percent may completely curtail that.

Spending 10 percent less money is likely to significantly improve your wallet and your financial health.

If you currently spend, say, 180 minutes of your workday being unproductive, switching out just eighteen minutes of that time into a task that is hyperproductive may have a huge impact.

Devoting 10 percent of the time you're physically together with your spouse/partner (or friends) to becoming more deeply connected emotionally could have a big impact on your relationship quality over time.

Experiment

In what domains of your life have you been perhaps devaluing the potential of small changes, or overlooking possible easy wins? What easy wins do you have available to you?

A hugely important skill in overcoming self-sabotage is being able to find simple, low-sacrifice, low-willpower solutions. The easiest solution is sometimes the smartest solution, even though our brains sometimes devalue those simple solutions. Making changes in your physical environment will subtly shift your thinking and behavior and help you collect easy wins. In general, make external, environmental tweaks before attempting harder, internal changes.

IS CHANGING YOUR THINKING ENOUGH?

A very common self-sabotaging pattern is believing that making thinking changes alone will lead to changes in your behavior. There often needs to be an intermediate step.

It's usually not: Recognition of thinking errors ➧ Behavior changes.

Rather it's: Recognition of thinking errors ➧ Design changes ➧ Behavior changes.

What I mean by *design changes* are environmental changes (like the ice cream example) and changes to your workflow and the systems and processes you use for decision making. This may sound a bit opaque at this stage but they're concepts we'll cover in a lot more detail going forward.

Quick Start Guide to Knowing What to Do

If you currently have a self-sabotaging habit that's at the top of your mind, but you're struggling to come up with useful solutions, here are some quick initial tips for doing so. This first set of troubleshooting strategies are about knowing what to do, and then we'll move on to tips for doing what you know—that is, successfully implementing your insights.

Recognize Cases in Which Acceptance Is Better Than Problem Solving

Sometimes what irks us doesn't actually need a solution. I'd like to be able to write flawlessly without countless drafts. I could jump to the conclusion that I need a solution that will allow me to write impeccably straight off the bat. However, fundamentally, trial and error is the nature of the work. The problem doesn't need solving so much as I need to accept that no book or article I write will be perfect in the first draft.

Relationship issues for which you're thinking, "How can I get my partner to be more/less . . .?" also often require accepting the reality of the situation rather than a strategy to get him/her to do what you want. For example, you'd like your partner to regularly take the lead in [insert your wish: taking out the trash, getting the kids from daycare, asking you about your day]. However, doing those things using their own initiative is not their nature. If the far easier route is accepting that you need to take the lead yourself, you don't need to solve the problem of how to get them to proactively do more of what you want. By recognizing and accepting this, you save yourself the aggravation of feeling like you're banging your head against a brick wall by unsuccessfully trying to change them. You're not taking responsibility because you think you *should*, so much as you're being pragmatic and realistic about what their nature is and how you react to that.

Experiment

Are there any situations where acknowledging reality, even if you wish it were different, could help you cross solving a problem off your list? Are there any problems you're seeing where someone else might say, "Why is that such a problem?"

Recognize If You've Already Thought of Good Solutions

Broadly speaking, many problems have a short list of potential solutions. For example, you're depressed. Your basic choices are try medication, try therapy, try a self-help book or program, try exercise, make a major change in your life (such as changing jobs), or do nothing. If you have a tendency to overcomplicate problem solving, you may be overlooking the fact that you've already thought of the best solution but you haven't accepted and implemented it yet. You may be overestimating how complicated implementing your solution needs to be. For example, starting therapy to treat your depression doesn't mean going and interviewing every therapist in town to find the perfect fit. It could involve simply calling a friend who saw a therapist they liked and asking for the therapist's name.

Recognize If You See Barriers That Don't Exist

Continuing with the depression example, let's say you'd like to try therapy. You know it's expensive. You see that as a barrier except that, realistically, you know you can afford it. You'd prefer not to have that expense, but you can swing it. Likewise, you see taking time off work for your therapy sessions as a barrier when you don't actually know if it's even a problem. You haven't gotten around to finding out whether the therapist you'd like to see offers evening or weekend appointments or to having a chat with your manager about whether you could get time off if necessary.

Sometimes all it takes to help you realize you're only imagining a barrier to problem solving is for someone to ask you, "If that's what you want to do, why don't you do it?" If there's no one around to do that for you, you might need to ask the question yourself.

Recognize If You've Solved a Similar Problem Before

You may already have the knowledge you need to solve your own problems, but you haven't managed to pull that information out of your brain and connect it to the issue at hand. If you're prone to *imposter syndrome* (see chapter 12) or you're a perfectionist who overcomplicates solutions, you may be especially likely to underestimate your knowledge. You might think you don't know how to tackle an issue when, in reality, you've already successfully solved that problem in another related, but perhaps not identical, context.

Always ask yourself what you already know that might be relevant to the problem at hand. Have you succeeded in solving a similar problem? Is that situation more similar to your current dilemma than you've realized?

You can also try asking yourself what solutions for other problems you've used lately. You may know that automating tasks using technology works well for you or that using physical reminders suits your personality and lifestyle. There might be a principle, strategy, or tool you find useful for thinking about work-related issues that you could apply at home, or vice versa.

Recognize When You Can Eliminate One Problem by Solving a Different Problem

Sometimes you need to solve a different problem from the one you're thinking about. I already gave an example of this from my own life: how taking breaks when I'm tired solves the problem of task switching, without directly targeting the issue of task switching.

If your current way of thinking about a self-sabotaging habit is only producing solutions you don't follow through on, that's an excellent cue that you need to think about the problem in a fundamentally different way.

Experiment

Try out the strategy of discussing a problem with a friend (or sibling, partner, etc.). This can be a fruitful technique for helping you see your problem in a new light. You might start the conversation with, "I'm trying to find a solution for . . ." Then share what ideas you've had so far. "The best idea I've had so far is . . ., but that's not quite right." The goal of this technique is mostly to stimulate your own thinking. If your friend makes any useful suggestions, that's a bonus. Try this with one of your current problems. If doing that isn't convenient right now, then start with identifying who in your life could potentially serve this role for you.

Quick Start Guide to Doing What You Know

Knowing what you *should* be doing to overcome self-sabotage is only half the equation. The other half is how you get yourself to do what you know. Here I'll provide a quick overview of common psychological roadblocks people encounter in implementing their solutions along with some tips for overcoming these. As you read, pay attention to the principles and not the specific examples. When it comes to the specifics, one person's light-bulb moment is another person's eye roll. However, the broad principles are much more universally relevant.

Replace Behaviors You Want to Do Less of with Behaviors That Require the Same Amount of Willpower or Less

You want to spend less time browsing the internet in the evenings. You think you would be better off working on a creative project; however, you don't make any changes. Clicking around on your computer requires virtually no willpower, whereas your creative project requires a medium to high amount of it.

Solution

Try making the assumption that whatever you're doing, that's the maximum energy, concentration, and willpower you've got at that particular time in your day and week. As a general rule, attempt to replace behaviors you want to do less of only with preferred behaviors that require the same amount of willpower or less. You can think of the willpower needed for an activity on a 0–10 scale (0 = none; 10 = max). If a behavior you want to reduce requires a willpower level of 2, don't try to replace it with a behavior that requires a willpower level of 4. We'll return to this topic in more detail in chapter 5.

Make the Best Thing to Do the Easiest Thing to Do

We can all make ourselves do at least a few behaviors that are very effortful or inconvenient. However, those should be the minority of behaviors we ask of ourselves. For the most part, you'll want to set up your environment so that the best thing to do is also the easiest.

Solution

Whenever you're not doing something you think you should be doing, always look first for how you can make your desired behavior easier rather than attempting to exert more willpower. For example, if you want to keep your car cleaner, keep a trash bag in the car so you don't throw trash on the car floor or stuff it into your car's pockets or compartments. If you want to wear a wider variety of items in your wardrobe, each time you put away your laundry, put whatever you've just worn at the back of your closet or drawer so that what you haven't worn recently is brought to the front, where you'll see it and grab it first. Or set aside outfits for the full week on Sunday rather than choosing what to wear each day. When we choose in advance, we tend to go for more variety, whereas when we choose in the moment, we're more likely to stick with the familiar.[3]

Many times tiny environmental or workflow changes easily reduce or eliminate problems, without requiring extra willpower. For example, I'm much better at not leaving pens lying around since I put a container for them in my living room and bedroom, instead of only in the kitchen. These are simple examples, but the principle holds true for more complex scenarios as well.

Plan for Obstacles to Success

A sound plan involves specifying exactly when and where you intend to implement it (for example, "I plan to go for a walk around the block each day after I've eaten lunch, provided it's over 40°F and the likelihood of rain is 30 percent or less") and preparing for, at least, the most likely obstacle to your success.

Use the if . . . then format to articulate how you'll bypass likely obstacles. For example, "If I have planned to exercise and I feel tired, then I will . . ."[4] Targeting the most likely obstacle is a good middle ground between planning for every possible thing that could get in your way and planning for nothing. *Defensive pessimists* have an advantage over optimists in planning for obstacles because it comes more naturally to them.[5]

Get Real About What You're Actually Willing to Do

Considering obstacles is a great way to make you aware of when you've formed a plan that involves behavior you're not actually willing to do. In particular, you want to catch a plan you might be willing to follow under ideal circumstances but not in real life. For example, most people are not willing to eliminate all white foods from their diet; therefore, that's a poor solution to weight control for the vast majority of people. You might think you're willing to give up all white food until you consider all the circumstances in which you're not, such as when you're at your favorite Italian restaurant, when your mom makes her famous cheesecake, and when someone brings birthday cake to work. When you start considering obstacles, you may realize there are too many for your plan to be realistic and that you need to reevaluate.

Get real with yourself about what you're willing to do. I like to think about this in three categories: behaviors I'm willing to do consistently, behaviors that I'm willing to do *sometimes* but not consistently, and behaviors I'm not willing to do. Here's an example:

> I'm willing to consistently go for a walk most evenings and make the more active choice when it doesn't require much extra time (for instance, take the stairs rather than the elevator, walk a mile

rather than take public transport, and park at the uncrowded far end of the parking lot).

I'm willing to sometimes do yoga, do the Couch to 5K program, play sports with friends, and try different types of exercise classes while traveling.

I'm not willing to work out at a gym or do a gym-like program at home.

You may not have to do the exact same behavior consistently to achieve the success you desire. Trying to force yourself to do that is a self-imposed rule. For example, there is no reason you can't do one type of exercise this month and another next month. There's no reason you can't eat vegan this month and paleo the next, if that's what you'd like to do.

Avoid Setting the Goal: "Make a Better Choice About . . ."

Have you ever noticed that if you frame goals by saying, "I'm going to make better decisions about . . .," you tend not to follow through?[6] Every time you ask yourself to make a decision about what to do and when and how to do it, you open yourself up to the possibility that the decision you make will be based on your current mood and circumstances rather than your long-term priorities.

Solution

When possible, decide once, and then set up systems and your environment to support you in following through, with the least amount of additional effort on your part. For example, if you've decided that a weekly date night would be good for your relationship but it requires organizing childcare, then you might make a standing booking with your babysitter for every Friday from 7:30 to 10 P.M. That way, you don't have to think about doing this each week; it's already scheduled in for you.

Recognize When You're Expecting More *of* Yourself without Giving More *to* Yourself

Because I've already mentioned how self-criticism traps people in self-defeating habits, I won't keep beating that drum. However, if this problem affects you, file away these additional tips:

> If you find yourself thinking, "I wish my partner [or other family member] were more supportive of my goal to do X," try giving that support to yourself instead. Ask yourself, "How can I be supportive of myself in the way I wish others would be?" If you want a cheerleader, be your own cheerleader. Look at the ways you're not currently your own cheerleader and brainstorm how you could improve that. What are the specific moments when you want a cheerleader and how can you provide it via positive self-talk? If you want more practical support, how could you facilitate that without waiting for permission or a proactive offer of help from someone else?

> There's a paradox in which if you gently and kindly remind yourself you're doing the best you can, you brain will respond with, "Well, you know what, I actually could try a bit harder." For example, you're trying not to yell, nag, or growl at your children. You acknowledge you're doing your best not to do that. In response to your self-kindness, your brain generates ways you could do better, and those actions feel achievable due to your self-compassionate mindset. This mind trick makes no logical sense given that if you were literally doing the best you were

capable of, you couldn't try harder than you already are. However, despite the logic flaws, this can be an effective strategy. Acceptance (and kindness) is often what opens up our minds to change. If you're a generally conscientious person, this method will most likely work for you. Give it a try.

Now that we've covered some of the psychology behind self-sabotage, we'll move on to practical steps for overcoming it. In the next few chapters, we'll discuss the foundation skills and habits you'll need to have the energy and clear mental space necessary for more complex changes.

Moving On

❏ What were your "that's me" experiences when reading the chapter?

Have you highlighted these in the book? Have you made your own notes or drawings about your insights? As previously mentioned, by making your own notes or flowcharts, you'll process the material more deeply and get more benefits from your reading effort. However, if highlighting (or any other more superficial approach) is all you've got the energy for right now, go for that option. If your default mode is to passively read, do anything that's better than that, even if it's not the absolute best approach.

A quick tip for the perfectionists out there: When I say write a few notes, I am not suggesting anything too onerous. For example, if I were to identify which patterns I can personally relate to from this chapter, my notes would look like this. "My patterns: I overcomplicate solutions; I underestimate how self-critical I am; trying to be perfect in all areas results in my getting overwhelmed and not taking simple actions." Done. Keeping things simple is a very important skill for most people who self-sabotage.

PART 2

....

Foundational Strategies to Recognize and Reduce Your Self-Defeating Behaviors

CHAPTER 4

· · · · · · · · · · · · · · · · ·

Pleasure and Self-Care

This chapter focuses on simple ways to add more pleasure and self-care to your life, which will lift your mood and make you more resilient to stress. Notice if you find yourself dismissing anything you read in this section because the ideas seem simple and you want to get on to "harder" stuff you think will be more useful or productive. That strategy often backfires and can significantly hinder your progress. If you're not doing the fundamentals well and don't take the time to master them, you start everything else with a shaky foundation and will be much more likely to slip back into your old patterns. *Overcoming self-sabotage is often about finding simple solutions to simple problems, even when those problems feel complex.*

Allow Yourself Experiences of Pleasure
· ·

A very common Catch-22 to keep an eye out for is the denial–binge cycle. Consider someone who's frustrated that they're not achieving enough, whether in their work and career or their projects around home. They deny themselves pleasure because they think they don't deserve it. However, by restricting their exposure to positive emotions experienced through fun activities, they deplete their willpower and emotional reserves and often rebound by overindulging in pleasure later (and then have less energy to devote to pursuing their goals). It's a self-perpetuating cycle. If you're doing a lot of self-sabotage and you're criticizing yourself for it, you're a prime candidate for thinking you're undeserving of pleasure. Here's a flowchart of this incredibly common pattern.

Frustration at not achieving enough

⬇

Sense of not deserving pleasure

⬇

Withhold treats and nurturing yourself

⬇

Even less energy to give to goal achievement + rebound
by overindulging in unhealthy treats

I'm not suggesting you should always shirk your work or other responsibilities in favor of constant treats and other fun distractions. Rather, it's important to get a mix of both. Allow yourself to take opportunities to experience simple pleasures, even if you think you don't deserve it. Because behavior influences thoughts and feelings, when you allow yourself to have more experiences of pleasure, you'll probably end up feeling like you're more deserving of it. However, if you constantly deny yourself experiences of positive emotions, you'll feel less and less deserving of these over time. Experiences of relaxation and positive emotions are rejuvenating, give your mind a break, and help you get a clear perspective on anything that's causing you stress.

The following five experiments will help you identify your current or potential sources of positive emotions.

(*Note*: In this chapter in particular, I give lots of my own examples to illustrate the concepts and kick-start your thinking. Specific examples are better than generic ones for making ideas clear, and sharing my own experiences helps me avoid the problem of including too many of other people's, who may not appreciate ending up in a book! There's nothing special about my personal examples, and some might even seem boring to you, but I hope their plainness illustrates how fundamentally simple your behaviors can be too.)

Experiment 1. What Feels Luxurious to You, Even Though It's Free or Inexpensive?

Sometimes even the simplest behaviors can feel like luxuries. What feels this way for you? Your answers should be very personal and strongly reflect your nature. You'll know you're keeping your list simple and personal enough if your responses resonate for you but might sound uninteresting to others.

To illustrate, here are a few super simple pleasures that feel luxurious to me.

Browsing a couple of aisles at Whole Foods or Trader Joe's in a leisurely, non-goal-directed way, rather than running in to get what I need and running out.

Long showers.

Listening to podcasts and audiobooks (the latter usually downloaded from my local library).

Going for an evening stroll.

Talking to my nephews and niece on Skype.

An afternoon nap.

Now, write down your own examples in your notebook, phone app, or whatever you're using for recording your thoughts.

Struggling to come up with your own ideas? If you haven't thought much about these types of questions before you may not immediately think of examples. It's okay if you accumulate your list over a period of a few weeks by adding items as you think of them. Write down your thoughts as they occur, so your insights don't hightail it out of your brain as soon as you're distracted.

Additional tips for experiments in this section:

Any of these positively toned self-reflection questions can be treated as a discussion topic for conversations with your family or friends. If you know someone very well, you may be able to think of examples that apply to that person more easily than they can think of their own ideas.

To the extent possible, include items on your list that you can do anywhere, in small bites of time. If you have pleasures you genuinely enjoy but are hard to fit into your life, ask yourself, "Is there a scaled-down version that doesn't require as much time or organization?"

Experiment 2. What, for You, Can Be a Pleasure or a Chore Depending on the Context?

Some simple pleasures can feel like a relaxing diversion or a total chore depending on the context. For example, we have a swimming pool. (This makes me sound richer and fancier than I am!) Cleaning the leaves out of the pool is something I find mildly pleasurable if I do it when I need a break from working inside on the computer. I get to enjoy the sunshine for a few minutes, and the physical exertion clears and calms my mind.

However, if it's one thing on a long list of weekend jobs I need to do, it feels like an unpleasant slog.

Here's another example: After I've been working intensively, driving to see friends or family (or even run errands) is a break, whereas driving places seems energy sapping at other times. Essentially any easier activity can be a reward or break from any harder activity.[1] Do you have tasks like this—that are relaxing if you do them in a certain way but are stressful or boring if you do them in another way? Write them down. Look for when you can do these activities in ways you find enjoyable rather than unpleasant.

Experiment 3. How Could You Link Simple Pleasures to Times in Your Life That Are Naturally Stressful?

Pairing pleasure with stress points can buffer you against the effects of that stress. For example, when I'm taking a flight, I pack peanut butter sandwiches. It's not a meal I feel like often, but once in a while I greatly enjoy it. It's now a very pleasurable aspect of flying. Because I've made it a routine, it's one less decision I need to make when heading to the airport.

What's a pleasure (perhaps one you don't want to overindulge in) that you could pair with an infrequent stressful activity? Another example of this principle is if you have a time of the week or month that's particularly stressful, such as, if you work for a magazine, the days leading up to finalizing each issue. What could you pair with these times to make them easier and more enjoyable and help buffer you against some of that stress?

Experiment 4. What's Pleasurable for You That, on the Surface, Doesn't Seem to Fit Your Personality?

Some of the joy that comes from simple pleasures is derived from the sense that you know yourself well and deeply understand what you like. We're all nuanced people. Everyone has a dominant nature as well as less dominant but still important aspects of their personality. Blended together, these are the elements that make each of us our unique selves. For example, one reason I enjoy travel is that I love having brief, friendly interactions with diverse strangers. It boosts my mood, and I enjoy the sense of serendipity. Travel facilitates having lots of twenty-second interactions with a very wide range of people. It's not obvious that I would enjoy this because I'm quite an extreme introvert. However, twenty-second conversations with strangers carry very little social obligation and can be an easy way for an introvert to get a fix of social energy without it feeling draining. I enjoy exploring the outgoing side of my nature this way. When you understand all the quirks of your nature and what you can enjoy, you can structure your life to include more opportunities to experience these mood boosts.

What's pleasurable for you that reflects a nondominant part of your nature? How does thinking about the range of behaviors and situations you enjoy help you understand your whole self, and not just the most obvious aspects of your personality?

Experiment 5. What Do You Think of as Your Purpose in Life?

When people put effort into and/or make progress toward what they see as their purpose in life, they subsequently feel a greater sense of well-being. This is true even when people are experiencing significant personal distress, such as in the case of people who have social anxiety disorder.[2]

Besides being good at your job, what do you see as your central purpose in life? For example, let's say you see it as being a good role model to others. What types of actions relate to this purpose? Which of these are achievable in your day-to-day life? In the case of striving to be a good example to others, you might see opportunities that relate to your kids and partner or in your neighborhood or workplace. Look for ways to combine pleasure and purpose, such as showing your children that having fun is part of a balanced life.

Problem Solve Anything That Gets in the Way of You Experiencing Pleasure

It's often the simplest, easily surmountable barriers that get in the way of us experiencing pleasure—for example, you get stuck in traffic and would like to listen to an entertaining podcast, but you don't have anything downloaded because your phone storage is full. What routines would help you keep your cabinet of available pleasures stocked? For instance, you might free up space on your phone every Wednesday when you're waiting to pick up your child from their piano lesson. Or you might set up your phone to do this for you, by automatically deleting photos and videos that have been uploaded to the cloud and deleting podcast episodes once you've listened to them.

Look at your answers to the prior experiments in this chapter to see if there are any easy systems or processes you need to put in place so silly little things don't get in the way of your ability to indulge in simple pleasures.

Practicing Self-Care When You're Feeling Uncomfortable Emotions

This section is about how to cope when you're feeling not-so-rosy emotions. It might not immediately be 100 percent clear why I've put this material in the self-care chapter. I've done so because having a sound plan for handling uncomfortable emotions will ensure you don't experience unnecessary amounts of these feelings and can work through them in a healthy and effective way, which in turn will help you feel better faster.

To take effective action when you're feeling a "negative" emotion you need to understand what each specific emotion is designed to help us do.

All emotions have evolved to benefit us in some way.* In some situations, a happy mood creates the best backdrop for optimal performance. However, a lot of research has demonstrated that, in other specific situations, uncomfortable emotional states, such as feeling a little stressed or pressured or feeling outraged at an injustice you witness, can produce the most creative thinking, the best decision making, the most persuasive arguments, and the most accurate performance. (See *The Upside of Your Dark Side* by Todd Kashdan and Robert Biswas-Diener for an excellent and entertaining look at the studies showing this.)

Let's do a quick tour of the major purposes of different types of feelings:

Anger energizes us and mobilizes us for action.

Anxiety makes us focus on details, puts us on the lookout for things that could go wrong, motivates us to do the right thing, and helps us avoid complacency.

Boredom lets us know that we need more novelty and challenge.

Doubt causes us to question what we're doing, mentally prepares us to accept change, propels us to work harder or differently, and can lead to us taking more cooperative approaches in dealing with people who disagree with us.[3]

---

* The relationship between our emotions and our thinking and behavior is often a system of trade-offs. Most emotions result in improvements in some types of thinking and worse performance in other types of thinking. This is relevant where safety is concerned—for example, driving during a panic attack wouldn't be recommended. Also, during arguments between romantic partners, it's common for one or both individuals to become what's known as *emotionally flooded*. In this scenario, it's usually better to step back and cool off, so you're able to think and act more rationally.

Envy, disappointment, and **loneliness** all provide information about what we want and when we've veered off track in terms of achieving that.

Feeling tired can lead to greater creativity and more authentic interactions because we're not as guarded when we're fatigued.

Guilt cues us to apologize and make amends and inhibits us from doing behavior that would trigger rejection or anger in others.

Irritation and **frustration** let us know our progress is slower than we'd like and that we may need to change our approach. These emotions also prompt us that something isn't sitting well and requires speaking out to correct it.

Sadness and **grief** cause us to pause, reflect, reevaluate, and think deeply about our values and what's important. Some cognitive skills, such as detecting lies, improve when people are in a sad mood.[4] And contrary to the popular stereotype, sad moods can enhance self-regulation.[5]

By understanding the positive purpose that underlies negative emotions, you can take them in stride more easily. They become less like something you need to urgently get rid of and more like a nonthreatening part of the human experience.

As well as overlooking the potential positive consequences of negative emotions, people often fear emotional discomfort because they overestimate its adverse impact. Specifically, people tend to overestimate how long negative emotions will last, overestimate what's necessary to change their emotional state, and vastly underestimate their capacity to experience negative emotions without losing control or long-term adverse consequences.*

The following is a strategy for coping with negative emotions. Although it may seem like there are a lot of steps, each one takes only a few seconds, and the routine will become relatively automatic with practice.

Step 1: Take Slower Breaths

Your emotions are how your mind interprets physiological signals from your body.[6] If your emotions have become too intense and you feel overaroused to the point that you can't think clearly, you can reduce your physiological arousal by slow breathing. Concentrate on breathing *out* very slowly and steadily (as if you were gently blowing up a balloon). When you slow your out breath, your in breath will take care of itself. Your heart rate and many other body systems will begin to return to a calmer state within approximately four to six slow breaths.

Step 2: Label Your Specific Emotions Accurately

Identifying your specific emotions makes them less overwhelming and helps you know what to do with those emotions. You need to be able to

---

* I'm not intending to be dismissive of those with clinical problems who need help recalibrating negative emotions that have become out of control and who deal with having a predisposition to that happening. Holding back from seeking treatment for clinical problems can be due to practical constraints, such as finances. However, not seeking help is also sometimes related to people overestimating what action is needed to handle emotions. Anxiety in particular is a negative emotion that, even when it has become very big and entrenched, can often be turned around extraordinarily quickly (see Kashdan et al., "Can a One-Hour Session of Exposure Treatment Modulate Startle Response and Reduce Spider Fears?"). For people who benefit from psychological treatments like cognitive behavioral therapy or acceptance and commitment therapy, the benefits usually start to emerge in the first month.

differentiate when you're feeling anxious, angry, ashamed, and so on. You can simply google for a list of emotion words, and pick what you're feeling from that list. If you have children, teach them to accurately and precisely label their emotions. Not only is it good parenting but it'll also increase your own emotion skills.

People who are better at granular understanding of their emotions are less likely to use maladaptive self-regulation (such as binging), react less to rejection, and have less anxiety and depression.[7] And kids who spent twenty to thirty minutes a week at school learning about emotion words improved socially and academically.[8]

Step 3: Accept Having a Mixture of Positive and Negative Emotions in Your Life

This may sound harsher than I mean it to sound, but you might find it helpful to remind yourself that you're not entitled to experience only positive emotions. As reviewed earlier, experiencing some emotional discomfort is *not* generally harmful and is in fact optimal. People do best when they experience a mixture of different types of emotions.

Being able to accept and tolerate feeling negative emotions opens up a world of possibility for what you can accomplish, allows you to choose the most meaningful path over the most comfortable one, and will help you reach your potential. For example, if you can tolerate uncomfortable emotions you won't need to avoid anxiety-provoking conversations. You'll be able to take meaningful actions, such as asking for what you want, even if you feel awkward.

If you don't fear that uncomfortable emotions will overwhelm you, cause you to become out of control, or lead to you doing something out of character, you'll be largely able to experience emotional discomfort without being distressed by it.

Step 4: Be Self-Compassionate About Whatever You're Feeling

Engage in self-compassion; in other words, don't criticize or beat yourself up for feeling something other than happy or content. Instead, give yourself some simple kindness by acknowledging the fact that you feel how you do and that's okay. Do this regardless of why you feel the way you do or what role you played in causing your feelings. You deserve that basic compassion.

Step 5: Determine if the Emotion Is a False Alarm

Doubt, anxiety, anger, guilt, and the like sometimes get triggered when there's no objective reason. Because emotions are designed to protect us from dangers and our emotional warning system is imperfect, having some false alarms is baked into the system. Sometimes it will be clear when your emotions are triggering a false alarm and sometimes it won't. Basically, if you're prone to experiencing a particular emotion very frequently, then you're probably getting false alarms.

Part of accepting the experience of uncomfortable emotions is accepting that you won't always know with 100 percent certainty when your uncomfortable emotions are a false alarm and when they're not.[9]

Step 6: Determine if the Emotion Is Providing Useful Information

Is the emotion telling you something about yourself or your situation? Can it help you take appropriate action? Ideas for optimal responses to different types of emotions are listed in the right-hand column of the table at the end of this section, on pages 71 and 73. Look to see what might be the best response to what you're feeling in your current situation. Don't treat the information in the table as gospel. Optimal responses to emotions are very context specific. The best approach is to stay cognitively and behaviorally flexible and choose your response based on the situation you're in.[10]

If it feels useful, you might want to develop a personal metaphor for reminding yourself that your emotions are there to serve you, point you toward the best decisions, and either energize or mellow your actions, depending on what's needed in a given circumstance. For example, you might think of yourself as an army general and your emotions as your loyal soldiers. Or you're the movie director and your emotions are your actors. Whatever works for you. Ask yourself, "What would help me understand that even my unpleasant emotions are present for the purpose of helping me succeed?" In any specific situation, your soldiers/actors might make bad calls, but broadly speaking, they're there to be of service to you.

Step 7: Identify Any Self-Sabotaging Reactions

Check for any self-sabotaging reactions (such as body language or tone of voice) that are preventing you from achieving your major goals. In the middle column of the table that follows, I've given broad strokes of the types of self-sabotaging behaviors people tend to do when feeling specific emotions. However, such a bullet point approach is oversimplifying. When people are experiencing negative emotions, their self-sabotaging thinking and behavior patterns often don't jump out and identify themselves. They're often subtle. For example, when you're feeling depressed or lonely you may not notice if your voice tone or body language change in ways that repel other people, even when that's not your intention. In fact, when people do personalized cognitive behavioral therapy with a therapist, one of the roles of the therapist is helping people identify the subtle self-sabotaging patterns they can't see themselves. Consider cognitive behavioral therapy as an option if, despite your best efforts, negative emotions seem to be having a harmful impact on your life. The book *Emotional First Aid* by Guy Winch is also a great resource for understanding common, self-sabotaging responses to negative emotions, with particularly strong sections for helping readers deal with loneliness and grief.

EMOTION	SELF-SABOTAGING RESPONSE
Anxiety	• Avoiding what makes you anxious and generally avoiding situations in which you feel uncertain. • Raising your self-standards and becoming more perfectionistic. • Overthinking and over-researching decisions; excessively delaying action.
Low Mood (Sadness or Depression)	• Withdrawing socially and from activities you'd usually find pleasurable. • Becoming more critical of other people. • Ruminating (overthinking, dwelling, wallowing, self-pity). • Skipping physical activity. • Becoming excessively pessimistic.
Anger	• Lashing out in ways that have the potential to cause harm to you or your relationships or to expose you to serious consequences (such as getting arrested for assault or vandalism). • Venting in ways that are cutting off your nose to spite your face.
Loneliness	• Becoming suspicious of others. • Developing an expectation that other people will be rejecting.

MORE USEFUL RESPONSE

- Use slow breathing to downregulate your physical arousal as needed.
- Recognize false anxiety alarms.
- Reduce avoidance (see chapter 6).
- Practice taking action when you don't feel 100 percent certain.
- Correct thinking errors, such as catastrophizing and personalizing.
- Rely more on your instincts for making complex decisions, especially where there are many options and there isn't a clear right or wrong choice.
- If anxiety becomes a problem, try cognitive behavior therapy or CBT-based self-help, such as my first book, *The Anxiety Toolkit*, or any of the free online resources provided by the Centre for Clinical Interventions (see http://healthymindtoolkit.com/resources).
- For anxiety issues related to relationships, see chapter 10 later in this book.

- Boost your mood through physical activity, pleasurable/meaningful activities, and approaching whatever you've been avoiding (see chapter 6).
- Use strategies to balance excessively pessimistic thinking, like imagining the best and most likely outcomes/explanations of situations rather than just the worst.
- For tips about coping with grief, see my article "How to Cope with Grief and Loss" (http://www.good.net.nz/article/coping-with-grief-and-loss).
- For a deeper understanding of the consequences of excessive pessimism, see chapter 3.

- Use feelings of anger to propel to you toward meaningful action—for instance, protesting personal or social injustice.
- Express your genuine (controlled) anger in situations in which doing so is persuasive to others, as in negotiations.
- Try seeing the situation from the perspective of the other people involved to make sure your reactions will serve your broader goals.

- Seek out meaningful relationships and interactions with others, including friendships and the micro-interactions we have with strangers and others we're not particularly close to (such as colleagues) throughout the day.
- Increase solo activities that give you pleasure so that being in your own company is more enjoyable.
- Increase pleasurable/personally meaningful social activities (for example, join a hiking club) so you have greater opportunities to interact with people who share your likes and values. Prioritize joining social groups that attract positive, friendly, energetic people.

EMOTION	SELF-SABOTAGING RESPONSE
Envy	• Avoiding people who trigger your feelings of envy;[11] — for example, not collaborating with people whom you see as more successful than you are. • Passive-aggressive comments. • Spending beyond your means and other keeping-up-with-the-Joneses behavior.
Boredom	• Engaging in behaviors that are numbing and distracting and designed to escape your emotions, such as excessive technology use, overspending, and overeating.
Guilt and Shame	• Lying, hiding, blaming others, defensiveness.
Regret	• Engaging in excessive shoulda, woulda, coulda rumination. • Being self-critical, or ruminating without taking any objectively useful actions. • Considering many options for preventing past mistakes from recurring but implementing none of them.
Frustration	• Giving up too soon or overpersistence, depending on your predisposition. • Getting irritated with other people. • Blaming other people or circumstances, and avoiding personal responsibility. • Not accepting reality—for example, someone shows you and tells you who they are but you keep thinking they'll change.
Doubt	• Engaging in socially transparent self-puffery. • Overthinking or overworking. • Avoiding feedback or responding angrily or defensively to feedback.

MORE USEFUL RESPONSE

- Support other people when things go right for them, such as when a colleague or a sibling experiences success.
- Learn from the people you envy. What are the strategies that make them successful?
- Balance distorted thinking if you underestimate the effort, trial and error, or personal costs involved in someone else's success.
- Ask yourself if you really do want whatever it is you feel envious about, such as a job that has much more responsibility or that involves constant travel.
- Do a reality check as to whether you're seeing only someone's successes (such as on social media) and not their failures or hardships.

- Seek out personally meaningful activities.
- Consider whether boredom is a result of needing to engage in more novel (new) and challenging activities.
- Check you're not overinvested in only one domain of your life—for example, being overly focused on work.

- Make genuine apologies and amends.
- Re-frame shame (global self-criticism about who you are) as guilt (remorse about specific behaviors).

- Identify the lesson you need to learn from your regret and put that into behavioral terms—for example, you didn't call the police about a suspiciously acting person and then you found out your neighbor was burgled. You might decide that, in future, you'll take action whenever safety is involved, even if it ends up being a false alarm. Perhaps you add the nonemergency police number to your phone contacts to make calling easier.
- Implement the single behavior you see as having the greatest potential return on investment for helping prevent similar regret; you can always implement other solutions later but start with what's most important, without getting excessively perfectionistic about it.

- Build your tolerance for frustration.
- Ask yourself if being more accepting of other people would reduce your feelings of frustration.
- Check in with yourself about whether your frustration is a sign of needing to change your actions or if it's a false alarm and you're already on the most meaningful and efficient path.
- Make sure low frustration tolerance isn't due to exhaustion.

- Seek feedback rather than avoid it.
- Step back and look at the big picture to see if you need to change your actions.
- Use strategies to uncover any blind spots.
- For more on self-doubt and the imposter syndrome, see chapter 12.

Experiment

What's an emotion you have tended to think of in a way that's wholly negative that you now see in a different light? Of the emotions listed in the table, which do you need to respond to more usefully?

Cycles of Diminishing Self-Care

Here's a principle everyone needs to understand about stress. When stress has a negative effect, it's often not the stress itself that directly causes the problems. Instead, the negative impact happens because stress disrupts the self-care we'd normally do. It's an indirect effect. Let's take a look at the pattern as a flowchart.

It's not usually: ➧ Stress ➧ Problems
Rather it's: ➧ Stress ➧ Skipping self-care ➧ Problems

Self-care helps us tick along with our lives and goals, while maintaining a positive mood most of the time. The absence of self-care can leave us feeling pretty terrible. For example, when I'm under stress, I sometimes skip my multivitamin, at the exact time I can least afford to be without the extra boost of energy and nutrients it provides. When I skip it and have less energy as a result, I make poorer choices, creating more stress and triggering a self-perpetuating cycle.

Three examples of how stress disrupts self-care routines:

De-Stressing: Anything that's a source of positive emotions qualifies as self-care if those positive emotions help buffer you from the effects of stress.

For example, you like taking a bath. It's a highlight of your day, makes you feel relaxed, and gives you a chance to decompress, but when you're busy, you skip it.

Socializing: Social withdrawal is common when people are under stress.

For example, you usually go out for Friday evening drinks with colleagues or friends. If you're tired you skip it, but it's something you enjoy that helps you debrief and transition from the workweek to the weekend and keeps you connected with friends.

Organizing: Planning and organizing keep your life or workday running smoothly. Skipping a step in your routine often increases your stress.

For example, you usually write a shopping list before going to the supermarket. If you're scrambling and too busy to write the list, you end up forgetting some of what you needed.

Here's an example from my own life: When I'm tired or stressed, I often don't use Google Maps as much as I should. I save a tiny amount of time and energy by not putting my destination into the maps app, but not using the app can end up costing me more time (and gas) overall when I miss a turn or when I'm driving to a familiar destination but don't know there has been an accident and an alternate route would've been a better choice.

Experiment

Which forms of self-care are the most important for you to prioritize when you're under stress? Try thinking of one example similar to each of the three examples given above. How can you increase the probability that you'll practice self-care even during tough times? If you're not sure how to make that happen, you'll likely have a few ideas once you've read the section on "Seemingly Minor Decisions" in chapter 7.

Know the Signs That You Need to Take a Break

An important form of self-care is knowing when you need to take a break.

Early Warning Signs

In chapter 3, I mentioned that the number one sign of when I need to take a break from working is that I start task switching—darting around from task to task without completing things. Do you know your own early warning signs that you need to take a break from working? To spark your ideas, here are a few more of my signs:

Losing concentration, making errors, or needing to repeat things—for example, needing to reread something because I wasn't fully concentrating.

Getting out of my seat every few minutes to do something that's unrelated to what I'm working on, such as walking to the fridge to get a cold drink or checking the mail. (Getting up to physically move around is very effective in boosting my energy but if I'm doing it too frequently, I know those energy boosts aren't sustaining me and I'm scraping the bottom of the barrel.)

Sneaking glances at non-work-related websites.

Experiment

Identify 1–3 of your early warning signs now. If you can't think of any, try asking someone close to you what his or hers are. Getting into a conversation on this topic can kick-start your own ideas.

Late Warning Signs

I think of late warning signs as indicators I've been chronically overworking and need a decent break to reset (such as a whole weekend off without email or errands). What are your key signs of sustained fatigue? Note that the same signs can also happen when you've been repeatedly avoiding work, leading to a buildup of anxiety. So if you've got avoidance tendencies, make sure your signs are from overworking rather than underworking!

These are some of my late warning signs:

Having low tolerance for anything frustrating.

Having exaggerated reactions to receiving small requests (for instance, getting an email request to do a very small favor and it feeling like it's a big deal).

Dropping food and drinks. If I've overworked during the day, I often find myself dropping or spilling food or drinks in the evening.

Experiment

Identify 1–3 of your late warning signs now. Repeatedly hitting the snooze button is an example many people mention. Get really personal and specific. Include examples like the ones I've shared, even if they are a little embarrassing.

Your "If This, Then That" Plan

Once you've pinpointed your early and late warning signs for needing a break, plan for how you'll respond when you notice those signs. Acting on your early warning signs is usually as simple as taking a short break as soon as you get the opportunity. Use the time to decompress, rather than multitasking on your break. For example, you could eat your lunch outside and leave your phone inside, to prevent multitasking.

As mentioned, what usually does the trick for me when I need a longer break is to have least one day of the weekend free from work, emails, or errands.

Experiment

Come up with your own "if this, then that" plan for what you'll do in response to your early and late warning signs. Make sure whatever you pick really is something you're prepared to follow through on and not something your "ideal self" might be prepared to do but your "real self" isn't. Once you've got a plan, can you foresee any obstacles to following through? Generate at least one idea for how you will overcome the main obstacle to you implementing your self-care plan.

What Are Your Signs That You're Taking Good Care of Yourself?

Just as there will be signs when you're stretching yourself too thin, there will also be signs when you're keeping your life in a nice equilibrium. For example, if I'm taking baths (my preference) rather than showers, that's a good sign for me that I'm allowing myself time to relax.

Experiment

Identify 2–3 signs that indicate that you're *not* overly stressed out.

Although some of the concepts in this chapter are basic, that doesn't diminish their importance. The more you practice self-care, the more you'll experience for yourself that doing so doesn't lessen your productivity. You'll find that a well-cared-for you effortlessly makes more good decisions that reflect the big picture than the stressed-out you who is being pulled in all sorts of directions and always running on empty.

Moving On

Try answering these questions before moving on to the next chapter. We'll keep this simple.

❏ What's the number one tip you want to remember from this chapter?

❏ What's one simple pleasure you'd like to integrate more into your life? What's the main obstacle to doing that? What solution would allow you to bypass this obstacle?

CHAPTER 5

· · · · · · · · · · · · · · · · · ·

Hidden Drains on Your Time
and Energy

Many of us go through daily life feeling exhausted and always playing catch-up. We repeatedly waste time (and other resources) because we don't have the mental energy up front to create streamlined processes for completing recurring tasks in an efficient way. The major theme of this chapter is to shift from expending most of your effort doing behaviors that pay off only once, to expending the most energy sowing seeds that are going to grow many plants. To put it another way, think about the conceptual difference of being a business owner as opposed to working in a business, except related to your personal life. To achieve what you want, put most of your energy toward the high-level strategies and development a business owner or an executive would do to move the company forward, not the repetitive tasks a lower-level employee would be charged with.

I'm Not Talking About Optimizing Your Life for Optimizing's Sake

· ·

Although this chapter may seem like it's about freeing up your time, what it's really about is freeing up your mind. When your mind is unnecessarily tied up thinking about your repetitive tasks, you won't have much attention available for thinking about the bigger picture. When you streamline your life, you'll be able to focus your energy in more meaningful ways.

When you reduce mental clutter and unnecessary busyness, you'll create a positive, upward spiral. Each time you create an easy, efficient process for handling a recurring task, you gain confidence in doing that. In combination, this confidence and energy give you more power and momentum to achieve even harder goals, which in turns boosts your confidence further. Let's check out this process as a flowchart.

You feel frustrated and exhausted from doing recurring
tasks inefficiently.

⬇

To turn this around, you create some efficient processes
for handling those tasks.

⬇

As a result, you get to spend less time and energy on those tasks.

⬇

Each time you use your efficient process, you're reminded what a
competent human you are. You're proud of yourself and gain confidence.

⬇

You're spurred on to solve more of your solvable problems. You're
confident in doing so. When you're in the habit of problem solving, you're
more likely to remember to do it, and with all the practice
you're getting, you're able to solve problems effortlessly.

⬇

The percentage of your life consumed by annoying,
recurring tasks shrinks.

⬇

You have lots of time, energy, and willpower for doing
whatever you want to do.

We Underestimate How Much Small Losses of Time (and Small Doses of Frustration) Add Up

The main cognitive pitfall to think about as you read this chapter is that we typically underestimate how little inefficiencies add up. Any one incident of spending ten minutes searching for a misplaced item isn't a big deal, but across a year (or a lifetime) that lost time and induced frustration become significant.

Let's look at the costs of poor workflow. If you're doing one thirty-minute errand per week that you don't need to be doing, that's twenty-six hours in a year. On a very microlevel, you can make tiny optimizations that add up to large savings.

As an example, each of the following actions adds up to approximately thirty minutes over the course of a year.

A five-second action you do once a day.

A thirty-second task you do once a week.

A three-minute activity you do once a month.

Small time/annoyance savers may seem meaningless at first glance, and ideally, you'd prioritize large time savings first; however, once you start looking, you'll see many, many opportunities to pick low-hanging fruit. A real-life example of this is that I now use a keyboard shortcut to type my email address into apps on my phone. When I type "qwe" (the first three letters on the top line of the keyboard) my email address auto-completes. By slightly optimizing the ways you do frequent activities, you'll reduce the drain repetitive actions have on you, and you'll gain free time for relaxing, playing, contemplating, spending time with others, or doing whatever else it is you crave.

The more awareness you have of how small amounts of time add up into large expanses, the more you'll naturally see opportunities to optimize the little tasks you do as you go about your day. You don't have to optimize everything, but you may as well collect all the small wins you can that don't require excessive effort or sacrifice.

Make the Best Thing to Do the Easiest Thing to Do

Back in chapter 3, I introduced the idea that a virtually surefire way to get yourself to do anything is to make the best thing, the easiest thing. Rely on your systems and processes, rather than your willpower. If the words *systems* and *processes* seem complicated to you, here's a very simple example to illustrate. My paper-recycling bin is right next to my mailbox, both of which are next to my front door. It's easier to dump junk mail directly into the bin than to bring it inside the house. It's also the best thing. When I write about figuring out an efficient workflow that fits with the rhythms of your day, this is the type of super easy process I'm talking about. There's nothing complicated about it.

Very small changes in workflow can make previously effortful behaviors effortless. A good example of this comes from a friend who lives in a two-story house with an upstairs bathroom. She gets her kids undressed for the bath downstairs where the laundry is, before taking them upstairs to the bath, so she doesn't need to bring their dirty clothes back downstairs.

Note: Everything you read in this chapter should feel like it reduces your effort rather than increases it. If anything seems too strenuous, take another look at the material to see if you've misunderstood or are overcomplicating it. The aim of the chapter is to help you make little adjustments that will make your life better and smoother. Shoot for making ultra-achievable slight improvements (which will cumulatively have a large impact), rather than trying to achieve Martha Stewart–level organization (unless that's your personality).

Strategies for Reducing Decision Fatigue and Streamlining Your Home Life

In recent years, much has been written about the heavy mental costs of constant decision making.[1] Decision making sucks up mental energy in the same way that resisting a delicious treat sitting right in front of you does. If you can free up your cognitive energy by eliminating unnecessary decisions, you'll be less overloaded, feel more relaxed, and have more zest for other activities. In the sections that follow, you'll find various categories of ways to cull excess decision making and streamline your home life. It would be overwhelming to try to comprehensively implement all of the ideas. You don't need to do that. Pick what seems most relevant. Or if you're looking for balance, implement one strategy from each category.

Create Master Lists

Master lists save unnecessary thinking and prevent forgetting. While it seems counterintuitive, an ideal time to create a master list is often just after you've finished an activity. For example, you might create a master packing list for travel by writing down what you take out of your bag when you return from a vacation or business trip. At that time, what you're glad you took, what you wish you'd brought, and what you wish you'd left behind will all be fresh in your mind. You can always add a couple of addenda for specific circumstances, like summer or winter travel. In some situations, creating a master list can be as simple as snapping a photo with your phone. For example, if you host an annual party or Thanksgiving dinner, you might take a photo of your grocery receipt after this year's big shop, so you can easily buy the same items next time.

Experiment
Thinking about your lifestyle, in what areas could creating master lists help streamline your life? Write those down so you will have notes to refer back to!

Write Yourself a How-To for Tasks You Do Infrequently

A master list is one type of how-to guide. There are also some other useful types.

When we do a task infrequently, we often forget how we did it last time. Due to *overconfidence bias*, we typically believe we'll remember how to do our infrequent tasks the next time they need doing, but we usually forget. This results in needing to figure the task out anew, repeatedly. I have a personal example of this problem that relates to my printer. Periodically, pages start coming out of the printer looking dirty, and I need to clean the drum. However, because this happens only a few times a year, I don't easily remember how to do it. Searching for the correct instructions is time-consuming and irritating. I now have the instructions saved in an email I wrote to myself with the subject line "How to Clean Printer Drum." This saves a ton of stress if I'm in a time crunch to print and mail a document. The time saved is valuable, but the stress saved is even more so. I don't need to think, Where did I find the information last time?

Another personal example is that once I've perfected a recipe and then stop making that dish regularly, I forget my own recipe. I think, Of course I'll remember, but I don't. In these types of situations, it's worth taking an extra couple minutes to write down what you did and to save that information in a place you'll remember.

Experiment

What do you do infrequently (every few months, seasonally, or annually) that you forget how to do each time? What do you periodically need to fix but forget how? How can you record this information to avoid the stress next time? Some categories to think about are computer/technology, home/garden maintenance, holiday-related tasks, or any equipment you forget how to use.

Store Information So It'll Be Easily Accessible at the Moment You Need It

Storing information so it's easily accessible exactly when you need it can help take the weight of remembering it off your mind. For example, I subscribe to an inexpensive service (called AwardWallet) that tracks my miles and points balances in airline and hotel programs, plus the expiration dates, membership numbers, and passwords. I no longer have to remember all the logins because they're all in one place, and I can see at a glance how many points I have and when my balances are expiring. With this information easily accessible, I'm more likely to remember to use the balances when booking travel, which saves me cash.

Similar to the printer example, the following are some other ways I use my email as the central repository for information I periodically need:

When I'm working on a book, I write myself emails with the subject line "a2b" for "add to book." When I think of any idea and I'm not in front of my computer at the time, I send myself an email with that subject line.

For stores I periodically call that have irritatingly long phone trees, I send myself emails with the sequences of numbers to press to bypass the options and get to a person.

I have my library card number stored in an email with the subject line "Library Card Number."

In some circumstances, the best option for where you store information may be to display it in your physical environment. In yet another printer-related example, I have a sign on the wall above the printer that says "prints on side facing down" for when I need to print shipping labels. Taping instructions inside cupboard doors is another great option for making information accessible exactly at the moment you need it, such as instructions for what should go where in the cupboard or how to use an item that lives inside.

Visual reminders and other how-to guides can be very useful for helping your partner (or children, friends, or co-workers) do tasks without needing to ask you.

I also love being able to set location-based reminders on my phone that trigger when I arrive or leave a certain location—for example, to remind me to take my reusable bags out of the car when I arrive at the supermarket. Because technology evolves so fast, I've put some other examples of ways to use technology to make your life easier on the book's website and also include some links for how to set up these handy shortcuts (see http://healthymindtoolkit.com/resources).

Experiment

Pick an area of your life in which having a visual reminder could help you reduce decision-making stress and decide when and where you'll create it.

Find Homes for Household Items That Match Your Workflow

As well as storing information so that it's accessible at the moment you need it, the same principle applies to how you store your physical stuff. Back in chapter 3, I gave the example of how I have containers for storing pens in multiple rooms of the house. Because I use scissors, tape, pens, and Sharpies frequently, I like to have a set of these in my bedroom, kitchen/living room, and car.

Having multiple copies of items you use frequently creates useful redundancy and can save you time and stress. For example, I find it handy to have two cooler bags so that when I'm running out the door to do shopping at least one of them will be easy to grab, instead of having to hunt for one. You may have the best intentions of putting items away consistently but if you don't always do that, having an extra provides a fail-safe.

Having a fail-safe also helps minimize the stress of having forgotten needed items. Instead of packing my toiletries every time I travel, I have a set that permanently lives in my travel bag. Also, several times a year I leave home to run errands but forget my purse. Therefore, I keep $20 in the glove compartment of the car for when this happens.

A final point you might think about for improving workflow around your home is scenarios where not owning the right tool for the job is costing you time and stress. Sometimes an inexpensive tool can make a job much easier, such as having a tape gun for packaging up boxes.

Experiment

Answer one of these questions:

What do you need to store closer to where you use it?

Is there anything you sometimes forget to take with you, so having a backup would be helpful?

What items do you use in more than one place, so having dupli-
cates in various rooms would be convenient?

Batch Actions

Which repeated activities would be more efficient if you batched them?
Here are a few examples of what I mean:

A friend who read a draft of this chapter decided to start
selecting five school outfits for her children at the start of
each week, rather than doing this every day for both her
children.

The same friend fills a large bottle with drinking water each day
and knows she needs to drink it by the end of the day to stay
fully hydrated.

When my daughter was eating baby food, I'd freeze it in ice cube
trays and then, once frozen, empty all the cubes into plastic bags.
This saved a ton of time compared to prying out one or two
cubes while holding the baby at the same time.

Once a year or so, I print out and cut up a sheet of address labels
for myself and my spouse.

Whenever I spot an ATM that dispenses $1 bills I get a stack of
fifty, so I don't run out when I need them for tips or bus money.
I also routinely get fifty $1 bills whenever I find myself at the
bank counter for something else. In combination, these
strategies prevent me from running out, and having too many
is never a problem.

Experiment
Answer either of these questions:

> What do you buy in quantities that are too small for your needs (such as baby wipes, hand soap refills, paper towels)? Purchasing what quantity of this item would save you from having to buy it so frequently, but still fit within your storage constraints?

> Thinking broadly, identify a situation in which batching would save you both time and stress.

Use Heuristics to Make "Good Enough" Decisions
A heuristic (in the way I'm using the word here) is any principle or guideline that produces a good enough result. It's similar to the idea of having a rule of thumb. There are lots of examples of how heuristics can prevent you from running out of items or having to do tasks unnecessarily frequently. Note that it's not assumed that heuristics will lead to making the right decision 100 percent of the time. They're aimed at balancing making the absolute best choices with reducing the mental load of decision making.

Heuristics can be especially helpful for decision making if you're prone to avoidance or overthinking. Here are a few examples of using heuristics to make good enough decisions quickly and painlessly.

> Because I tend to be an "under-buyer,"[2] I have a heuristic that I purchase 50 percent more of anything than what my brain tells me to buy. For example, instead of buying four yogurts, I'll grab six.

> If I've thought about buying an inexpensive item three times, I pull the trigger and order it online rather than thinking further.

Likewise, if I've thought "I need to . . ." three times, I do it right away. I don't literally count the times I thought about a task, I approximate by asking myself, "Have I thought about this more than once before?"

With writing, if I've spent ridiculously too long on a particular section, it almost always means the passage should probably be deleted rather than reworked.

If I'm overwhelmed by my to-do list and want to pare it down, sometimes I ask myself, "Would I pay someone to do this?" to evaluate whether an activity is worth doing. If the expected return from doing a task is so low it wouldn't warrant paying someone to do it, that's a good indicator it's not worth doing myself.

Author Chris Guillebeau has discussed the $10 rule he uses when traveling: If paying more, but by less than $10, saves stress, that's an automatic yes.[3]

My general rule is that tasks worth over $100 get done before tasks worth less than $100. I use the same heuristic for both home- and work-related tasks—for example, returning a $100 item that didn't meet my needs gets prioritized over returning a $10 item.

My family knows that, as a general rule, 7–8 P.M. is a good time to ask me any tech-support questions (or anything else I need to think about) because it's still early enough that I'm not trying to wind down for bed, but it doesn't disrupt my workday.

I use a variation on the one-minute rule.[4] The gist of the one-minute rule is that if you think of something that needs doing and it'll take less than a minute, you do it straight away. I interrupt what I'm doing only if forgetting would set me up for future stress—for example, if I think of something I need to put in my purse and forgetting that item would create stress. If forgetting wouldn't generate future stress, I don't interrupt what I'm doing. It's also probably more a three-minute rule for me.

A friend uses this strategy if she is having difficulty finding exactly what she wants (for example, when researching Airbnb apartments): She removes one of her criteria to introduce more flexibility. She says this helps her prioritize and makes her realize that what seemed necessary may actually just be desirable.

If you've read or heard about a heuristic someone else uses but it doesn't gel for you, you may just need to frame it slightly differently. For example, I find it difficult to put a dollar value on my time, but "Do > $100 tasks before < $100 tasks" works for me.

Experiment

As a way of generating further ideas, have a conversation with a friend or family member about the heuristics you each use in your everyday life.

Alternatively, identify a heuristic you've read or heard about and are interested in, but haven't implemented yet. Could you reword it, or change it slightly, so that it's easier for you to implement?

When There's No Major Downside, Use the "Ready, Fire, Aim" Approach to Improving Your Systems

If you tend to delay decisions due to anxiety or perfectionism, you may find yourself adding "Make a decision about . . ." or "Find solution for . . ." to your already overflowing to-do list. The popular ready-fire-aim principle refers to taking action now (ready, fire) and tweaking later (aim) if needed, rather than delaying.

Here's a personal example. I have two containers on my kitchen windowsill above my sink. One is for quarters, and one for any coins that aren't quarters. They're old takeout containers and were never meant to be a permanent solution. However, the fact I haven't gotten around to finding nicer containers is a good indicator that if I'd waited to implement a solution until I had pretty containers, I still wouldn't have done it. Now, I always have quarters when I need them and don't have a purse full of coins.

Although I didn't end up completing the "aim" component in the coin container example, sometimes you will need to adjust your solutions to get them working for you. It may be a only small adjustment that turns a problem-solving failure into a success. For instance, I purchased extra charging cables so I could charge my phone in whatever room I'm in, without having to hunt for a cable. However, I still found that whenever I was in need of a cable I could never easily find one. To fix this, I wrote "bedroom," "living room," and "car" on three sticky labels, and wrapped a label around each cord. This way, whenever a cord migrates away from its home base, I know where it needs to go back to.

Experiment
What's a workflow problem that you're delaying solving that could be solved now?

Alternatively, if you've tried to improve your workflow in a particular way and your solution isn't working well, how could you tweak that solution?

Pick When You're Going to Do Annual or Semi-Annual Activities
For certain items, buying them at the right time of the year will save both hassle and money. For example, I've set an annual reminder at the end of

summer to buy a new swimsuit and throw out the old one. There's a yearly window when they're on sale, but before they disappear from stores completely.

Pick when it makes most sense for you to do tasks you do annually, semi-annually, or seasonally (such as pest control). How do these tasks best fit into the rhythms of your life? For example, if you'll need to make a phone call, when in your week do you typically have the time and social energy for that? Holiday weekends can be a good option for doing certain seasonal activities, especially because sales often occur on holiday weekends (Labor Day weekend is a good time to look for a swimsuit replacement).

As well as using this strategy for necessary jobs, you can also use it to ensure you do activities you *want* to do, that you might not get around to otherwise. For example, let's say you want to make a tradition of having a party at your home each year to mark the beginning of summer. Pick a date for the party (the third Sunday in June), and another date for when you'll send out the invitations each year (the last Monday in May).

Google Calendar is an excellent free tool for creating recurring calendar reminders. Decide how often you want to do tasks like getting a haircut or oil change. Use automatically recurring calendar reminders so that you don't have to repeatedly put the item on your calendar. You can do the same for annual tasks like "order Christmas turkey." Include as much relevant information with the calendar event as possible, like the phone number for your mechanic or hairdresser. By removing the extra step of needing to look up the phone number, you make it less likely you'll ignore the reminder when the event notification pops up in your email or on your phone.

Experiment

Set up one automatically recurring calendar reminder using your calendar system of choice. If you don't have a system, try Google Calendar. Check the Repeat box when you create a calendar event.

Identify Unnecessary Repetition

Are there phone numbers you repeatedly have to look up because you don't have them in your contacts? Do you set your alarm each evening, instead of having your phone programmed to do that for you? Do you manually back up your photos from your phone to the cloud, instead of having that on autopilot? Are there bills you don't have set to autopay?

There are all sorts of little actions we do repeatedly when set-and-forget options are available. Realistically, if you haven't already done these tasks, it's likely something is getting in your way. What seems like it should be easy may need a bit more figuring out. Maybe you lost your login and can't get into your online account for your electric company to set up an autopayment? Maybe you don't know how to automatically back up to the cloud? For these types of roadblocks you may need to take a "pay yourself first" approach and set aside some time for doing this work, before you start your regular workday. Recall the principle from the outset of this chapter to spend most of your effort on activities that will pay off repeatedly rather than only once.

Retrain Decision Leeches

Do other people offload decision making onto you? Because decisions drain mental energy, it's smart (and crafty) to outsource making choices to other reliable decision makers whenever possible. If you're a sound decision maker, other people (at home or work) may try to get you to do more than your fair share. Examples of group decisions left to you could be meal and restaurant choices, family finances, decorating, shopping decisions, and whether to say yes or no to an opportunity.

Sometimes other people's methods are sneaky. For example, a family member is in charge of a decision. Instead of following through themselves, they email you links to all the possible choices for your opinion. It's easy to get sucked into the trap of helping because it's not a big deal.

You may feel flattered or important when people ask for your help. However, over time, leaving decision making to you will become their habit. Your lovable decision leeches may even lose confidence in making decisions without your input. Decision makers often feel a big sense of responsibility for the outcomes of their choices. By sharing the decision making, you share this responsibility load with other people and liberate yourself from excess responsibility.

How can you retrain others to do their fair share of decision making? Try this. When someone asks for your help with a decision, push it back to them. If other people have entrenched habits of leaning on you, you may have to be quite direct. For example, you might (nicely) say to your spouse, "I don't mind what decision you make but I'd like you to make the decision. I'd like you to be in charge of this, without input from me." When possible, empower others' confidence in their decision making. If you have any preferences for what decisions they make, keep your requirements list short, such as, "I don't mind what washing machine you buy for us, as long as the capacity is at least . . ."

Experiment

Have you been taking too much responsibility for decision making? Identify one person in your (home or work) life who needs to be empowered to make more decisions on their own and make an effort to practice that with them.

How Do You Fit Developing Systems and Processes into Your Life if You Feel Exhausted?

If you're completing your recurring tasks in inefficient ways, that can easily suck up hours of your week and trigger your ingrained self-sabotaging behaviors. It's mentally exhausting and interpersonally stressful if, for example, you find yourself yelling at your kids because you can't find something you need as you're heading out the door. On the one hand, correcting these patterns becomes a virtuous circle in which, as you free up your mental energy, it becomes easier and easier to do more of that. On the other hand, if you already feel stretched to breaking, how do you know where to start?

Where you might go wrong in applying the tips from this chapter is trying to squeeze life strategizing in on top of everything else you're already doing. Life advice often includes an incredibly long laundry list of all the things we "should" be doing daily. Who could possibly fit in all of these: personal mindfulness, mindful parenting, exercise, home cooking, yoga, meditation, investing in relationships, staying on top of cleaning and tidying, and leaning into our careers and not be exhausted at the end of each day?

Let's go back to the idea mentioned in chapter 3 that you can rate how much willpower (or cognitive effort) a task takes on a scale of 0–10. As stated, let's assume that whatever you currently do at a particular hour of the day is all the cognitive energy you've got in that time zone. If you want to do more of a behavior, slot it into your life during a time when you already do activities that take that much willpower.

One solution you may not have considered is that slotting in new behaviors can be a temporary switch. For example, you might decide to take a week off from cooking, stock up on microwave meals, and do some life strategizing instead. Or if you have some flexibility in your workday, you might take some of your time to do a task that straddles work and personal spheres. As a self-employed person, it took me ages to recognize that when a task has both career and personal elements, it's okay to do those tasks during my workday.

If you have too many priorities that you consider high, those priorities may need to take turns. Life gets out of balance when we *always* prioritize certain behaviors and *always* de-prioritize others. It's desirable to skip your yoga class once in a while to focus on another high priority behavior that day, without worrying that you're going to completely abandon yoga by doing so.

If you find that you still get distracted by the internet, even during your periods of peak energy, you could try temporarily turning on an app like StayFocusd, which I'll also mention in chapter 13. This handy tool is a free extension for the Chrome web browser and is available through the Chrome web store. It will block certain websites after you've used them for a set amount of time. You pick the sites and time limits. Try using StayFocusd for a week or two to allow yourself extra time and concentration for life strategizing. See http://healthymindtoolkit.com /resources for more about how to set it up.

Another solution involves getting support from others (for example, hiring a babysitter to watch the kids more often or asking a co-worker to take on an extra project at work) so you can devote more of your time and energy to life strategizing. Prioritize using time when you have support available for implementing strategies that will keep paying off for you repeatedly, rather than using it for behaviors that are valuable but pay off only once.

Having a buddy who is also working on streamlining their repetitive tasks can be hugely helpful too. Who do you know who might also want to work on implementing the concepts from this chapter? Share your existing strategies and any new strategies you try out to inspire and invigorate each other.

Experiment

Part 1: Assign your daily/weekly activities to a willpower category as in the following example. The sample activities may fall into a different willpower category for you.

Willpower/Cognitive Energy Required (0–10)	Activity
Willpower level 0–2	Watching TV, browsing online, eating mindlessly
Willpower level 3–4	Going for a stroll, eating mindfully, cooking a meal that's already partially prepared (such as reheating leftovers and making a salad)
Willpower level 5–6	Cooking from scratch
Willpower level 7–8	Vigorous exercise, discussing a topic of conflict respectfully, fixing a problem that has been hanging around a while
Willpower level 9–10	Resisting junk food or alcohol that's sitting right in front of you

Part 2: How much cognitive energy do you think you'll need available to do the type of life strategizing mentioned in this chapter? Based on your activities chart, which activities could you potentially sub out temporarily? For me, I need around level 5–6 for life strategizing. Therefore, I can sub this into my day wherever I currently do an activity that takes a 5–6 cognitive energy or above.

The best news: Over time, the more you put streamlined processes in place, the more hours in the day you'll have level 5+ cognitive energy. This is the virtuous circle concept I mentioned earlier.

Moving On

Try answering these questions before moving on to the next chapter.

❏ Of the ten general ways you could reduce excess decision making and streamline your life, which seemed most relevant to you?

❏ What's a convenient home you could create for one of your currently homeless items, right now, in the next couple of minutes, without adding that task to your to-do list (as in the coin containers example)?

CHAPTER 6

....

Strategies for Overcoming Procrastination and Avoidance

W e've all experienced the nagging dread and anxiety that accompanies procrastination. Procrastination (avoiding specific tasks) and avoidance (a more general pattern) can also cause problems in relationships, especially if you make a habit of avoiding or you routinely ask others to do things for you.

For anyone who feels like they are getting in their own way, there's a very high chance that avoidance is a big part of the problem.[1] Avoidance creates stress, increases anxiety about whatever you're avoiding, and sucks away self-confidence. Like perfectionism, avoidance creates a Catch-22. Having an avoidant coping style is self-sabotaging and impedes overcoming self-sabotage. For example, a family member recently told me she avoids making to-do lists *because* she knows they work extremely well for getting her started on avoided tasks and it feels easier to stay stuck.

We all have things we feel overwhelmed by. Therefore, everyone needs a personal toolkit of strategies for breaking through procrastination and avoidance.

21 Strategies for When You're Procrastinating

What follows is a huge list of strategies for breaking free of avoidance. One person's favorite tip will be someone else's least favorite, so I've given you lots of ideas. The more strategies you're comfortable with, the more likely it is that, for any given situation, you'll have an option in your toolkit that fits your needs and that you feel capable of using in that instance. Therefore, try to find at least five strategies you're open to.

Train yourself to think, "What strategy could I use?" whenever you're avoiding something. You can also use this list as a reference guide and come back to it when you need fresh ideas. You may even notice that your favorite go-to strategies shift over time (mine do).

Experiment

As you read through the list of strategies, identify what you already know works for you and what you're prepared to try. Mark the strategies as follows:

I = I know works for me.

P = Prepared to try it.

N = Not prepared to try it.

If you're in a relationship, compare notes with your partner to understand which strategies appeal to each of you.

1. Write a To-Do List for Each Current Project, Rather Than Putting All Your Tasks on a Daily To-Do List

When you use a daily to-do list and your day gets hijacked by circumstances, it's demoralizing to keep moving items over to your next day's list. By writing all the actions you need to take for a particular project on a list that's just for that project, you can work through your tasks as you have time.

Project specific to-do lists also help you use scraps of time effectively. For example, if you have a spare five to ten minutes, and there is a five-to-ten-minute job on your list, you can quickly see that option. Save your daily to-do list for things that truly need to be done that day (like "Put out trash" because tomorrow is trash pickup day).

2. Practice Making a Good Enough Decision

When you're facing a complex decision that involves lots of options and variables, try briefly reviewing your choices in a deliberate way, and then allow your instincts to guide you toward a final choice. Holding lots of information in mind overwhelms our conscious thinking processes. Do brief conscious deliberation, and if no clear winning solution emerges, sleep on it or do an activity in which your mind can wander (take a shower, go for a walk, or drive somewhere). When you do this, your brain will keep unconsciously working on your problem in the background and may provide you with an epiphany or an instinctive cue of which direction to take.

In reality, neither endless amounts of careful consideration nor instinctive judgments are going to produce the right decision 100 percent of the time, but research has shown that relying on instincts can actually produce superior choices in some cases, and it's certainly less mentally taxing.[2]

3. Identify if a Self-Inflicted Rule Is Causing Your Avoidance

When you find yourself thinking, I have to do X to get this done, take a moment to check if that's completely true or if it's just a rule you've created for yourself. These types of rules are very, very sneaky in that we often fail to recognize when we've simply self-generated a rule. For example, you're avoiding starting your Christmas baking. You have a self-imposed rule of "I have to bake three types of cookies for Christmas." Who says Christmas requires three varieties and not one, two, or four? Can you simplify your expectations? Maybe one type of cookie is fine.

4. Decide *Not* to Do an Item That Has Been Hanging Around on Your To-Do List

The strategy of removing undone items from your to-do list gets back to the issue of prioritizing. For example, one of my hobbies is accumulating (and spending) miles and points for travel. There are a huge number of deals for earning extra miles that come along. Trying to participate in all of them is overwhelming. It also has a big opportunity cost because chasing small deals gets in the way of doing much more productive activities.

It can be difficult to decide *not* to do something that has some value but isn't a priority. However, it's empowering and can give you the confidence boost you need to get unstuck with whatever *is* a priority. Decide to permanently *not* do something that's on your to-do list. Pick a task that, even though it's valuable, does not have the return on investment (ROI) of other options.

5. Get a Boost by Boosting Someone Else

When people express positive emotions, they feel more positive emotions. For example, when you express enthusiastic happiness for a colleague or family member who has experienced a recent success or you express gratitude, you get a boost too. Why is this a strategy for overcoming avoidance? "Negative" emotions signal danger, whereas positive emotions signal safety.[3] When we feel safer and the world seems like a kind and hospitable place, we're more likely to explore. We're wired this way through evolution. Exploring is the opposite of avoidance, and exactly what we're aiming for.

6. Determine if You're Avoiding as a Way of Rebelling

If you've been resisting someone else's advice, suggestions, or nagging, but your resistance isn't in your own best interests, connect doing the behavior you're avoiding with a personal value that's important to you. For example, food has become buried in your freezer. You're avoiding clearing it out, which your spouse has been nagging you to do. Ask yourself, Why do I need to do this task for me (as opposed to for whoever is pushing you)? Your answer might be this: "I value my time. The more cluttered the freezer is, the more of *my* time I'm going to spend looking for items in the back." Connect the avoided behavior to whatever value is most motivating for you personally. Examples of potentially relevant values (depending on the situation) include aesthetics, saving money, saving time, optimizing/efficiency, safety, expressing your love through action, do unto others, or minimizing waste.

7. Pretend You're Going to Outsource the Avoided Task and Write Directions

If you're avoiding a task, imagine that you've assigned it to another person. Write instructions that contain enough detail for someone else to successfully complete the task. How does this strategy overcome avoidance? There are a few different ways this works. Here are four: (1) Imagining someone else doing the steps of a task can make you realize you're capable of those steps. (2) Thinking through outsourcing can help you get the psychological distance you need to break free of avoidance. (3) You may have more reasonable expectations of others than of yourself. When you design a task for someone else, you may naturally make it easier and, consequently, less likely to trigger your avoidance. (4) Planning out the steps involved in a task takes cognitive effort. Once you've done that work, the rest of the task may seem much more achievable and not worthy of avoidance.

8. Try searching Google, YouTube, or Pinterest

Turn to the internet for help. For example, if you're avoiding writing a résumé, use Google to search for "résumé writing tips." If you're avoiding packing for a trip, search "packing list for [destination]" on Pinterest. Even if you don't really need help with figuring out how to do a task, you may pick up good ideas or just feel less alone in whatever you're trying to accomplish. This strategy may sound a bit silly, but it can be surprisingly effective. Taking the tiniest amount of action can help you move past avoidance. Give this one a try, even if it sounds very basic to you. It's especially useful when you feel like you don't have the energy for other strategies or your avoidance has built up so much that other strategies seem daunting.

9. Limit How Long You Work on an Avoided Activity

For example, commit to working on an avoided task for fifteen minutes minimum, but set a maximum of an hour. Limit setting can prevent boom and bust cycles of action–inaction. If it has taken you a long time to get started, there's a temptation to overwork once you do start, but overdoing it just sets up a negative cycle.

10. Break Your Own Rules

Remember that it's okay to break your own rules. If you normally don't work on Sundays or don't work past a certain hour of the night, sometimes shaking things up and breaking your own restrictions can help you move past avoidance. If you've finally gotten into a task after putting it off, it's often not a bad idea to keep going with it for a while, even if that results in sacrificing some down time. However, you still want to cap it, as mentioned in strategy 9. Sticking with your avoided activity for one hour is less likely to trigger boom and bust cycles than working for three hours.

11. Ask for Help

Are you trying to solve a problem yourself even though you have a customer support option available? Are you overlooking an option to call, email, or tweet for help? Likewise, are you attempting to solve a problem yourself even when someone in your social or work network might have useful ideas?

IMPORTANT!

If you're very avoidant, make sure asking for help doesn't become a strategy to avoid figuring anything out yourself. If asking for help too soon is an avoidance strategy for you, you can create some type of guideline to determine when and if it's time to get outside assistance. For example, you commit to trying three of your own ideas before asking for help.

12. Teach Some Aspect of Whatever You're Stuck With

The idea of teaching to bypass avoidance mostly applies to work tasks. Create educational material for your colleagues, employees, boss, or students (whatever applies in your situation). For example, if you're a programmer who's avoiding doing a difficult or laborious coding task, you might write up a cheat sheet or make a video for how to do a related task you feel confident about, in the most streamlined way possible.

Another take on this strategy involves teaching your child a skill. For example, if you're avoiding something to do with money management, teach your child some financial concepts you're confident with.

Because actions affect thoughts and feelings, acting confident and competent will typically make related tasks feel much more within your capacity.

13. Move Yo' Body

Physically moving your body, whether it's walking to the mailbox, shifting some boxes, or going running, kick-starts your thinking and your energy. Sometimes even walking to the fridge to get a cold drink works for me! (As I mentioned in chapter 4, if I find myself doing that repeatedly in a short space of time, it's usually a sign that I need a proper break.)

14. Have Fun with the Idea That You've Become a Master of Avoiding

Some people are absolute masters of avoidance. They find ways to justify, excuse, or blame others for all their avoiding. They're expert contortionists in explaining why, on a case-by-case basis, they haven't done whatever they're avoiding. My personal expert avoidance skill is not disciplining myself to do jobs that objectively should be much higher priority than other jobs. I busy myself with all sorts of tasks of minor or medium importance and, all the while, important jobs roll over from one day's to-do list to the next, sometimes for weeks. My $100+ jobs first heuristic, mentioned in the last chapter, works well, but I stick to it only about 50 percent of the time. It works, but not perfectly, and I'm mentioning this to make the point that strategies don't need to work all of the time or even *most* of the time to be valuable.

It's hard to explain, but there is a psychological sweet spot where you can lightheartedly acknowledge how good you are at justifying your avoiding, but still take responsibility for making better choices. Experiment with different types of self-talk that are both self-compassionate and responsible until you find what works for helping you move past your avoidance.

15. Start in the Middle

If you feel intimidated by whatever the next step in your avoided task would normally be, pick another step that feels less daunting. Having project to-do lists (strategy 1) helps you easily pick a step in the project that feels manageable and fits with your current mood and concentration levels.

16. Clear the Decks

Clearing the decks is one of my personal favorite strategies. If you've been avoiding a task for a while and it's really important, try completely clearing your day. Make a deal with yourself that once you've done the action you've been putting off, the rest of the day is yours to do whatever you feel like. Note that I don't necessarily mean you'd spend ten hours watching Netflix. You could do that or you could do whatever productive work or personal tasks you felt like doing, and treat yourself to doing those tasks at a relaxed pace.

This strategy is recommended for when you have an extremely important job you keep putting off—for example, signing up for health insurance.

17. Correct Distorted Thinking to Overcome Anxiety-Induced Avoidance

Expecting your actions will have negative outcomes is almost guaranteed to trigger avoidance. Let's say yesterday you found your work a slog, you couldn't get into a good flow, and nothing came easily to you. That doesn't necessarily mean it will go the same way today, even if you're picking up exactly where you left off. If you can recognize yourself thinking, "This is going to be hard" or "This is going to be difficult," try remembering that you could be wrong.

A cognitive bias that can lead to feeling overwhelmed is thinking you need to do everything or do everything *now*. It's easy to overestimate how much you can get done in one day but underestimate how small amounts of regular work and effort add up hugely over longer periods. As author Chris Guillebeau writes, "We overestimate what we can accomplish in a day, but underestimate what we can accomplish in a year."[4]

Here's another common pattern that can happen with creative projects. You feel good while you're working on your project. However, once you've stepped away, you get a creeping anxiety that the work you've done is terrible. When you eventually get back to working on the project, you're pleasantly surprised that you've in fact done a lot of good work or gotten farther than you remember. However, when you underestimate the amount or quality of work you've done so far, you're more likely to put off getting back to it.

Whatever your personal thinking patterns are that trigger avoidance, you'll want to understand them enough that you notice when they're occurring. You can then learn to remind yourself to not completely trust those thoughts.[5]

My first book, *The Anxiety Toolkit*, deals with the thinking patterns involved in anxiety-induced avoidance in a lot of detail, so that resource is available if you need it.

18. Be as Clear as You Can About What Is and Isn't Avoidance

Here are three situations that look like avoidance but can be seen differently:

It sounds ridiculously obvious but avoidance is pausing *before* working, and taking a break is what you do *after* having done some work. You may be mislabeling certain behaviors as avoidance because you don't recognize the value of taking long breaks from some types of tasks. For example, sometimes taking several weeks (or even months) off from a project allows you to come back to it with a fresh set of eyes and new insights. Even if you think a two-day break should be enough, that might be more of a wish than reality for some types of projects. Giving yourself permission to take a longer break can help you overcome avoidance because it allows you to break free of ruminating about whatever it is you're not working on right now. Maybe you need that extended hiatus to come back with a fresh perspective.

People sometimes also think they're avoiding when they're deliberately just prioritizing other things.

You may label yourself as being avoidant when it's more accurate to say that you don't want to do whatever it is you're apparently avoiding. Let's say you have a successful business and other people are repeatedly telling you that you could easily franchise, upsize, grow your business, and so on, but you'd prefer not to. Likewise, maybe you've been avoiding going to the gym but you actually hate the gym, so why are you attempting to make yourself go? There can be a lot of power in identifying when you just don't want to do the activity.

When you stop feeling guilty about your choices, you'll have more mental space to tackle forms of avoidance that you're motivated to change. One of my most personally empowering decisions was that I was never, ever going to try to attain magazine-cover abs. That decision makes me smile whenever I see a naked torso on the cover of the magazine. I think to myself, "That's something I never have to do."

19. Project Ahead to Imagine How You'll Feel Once You're Done (Maybe)

Imagining yourself feeling relaxed and happy once you've completed a task can be very motivating in some circumstances. However, this strategy can either work or completely backfire. There's some research evidence showing that when people visualize success, it can reduce the work they put in.[6] Visualizing success can lead to you mentally crediting yourself for work you haven't done yet. The only way to know for sure if this strategy will help or hurt you is to experiment and judge by your results. I find it helpful to imagine enjoying an evening of relaxation knowing an avoided task is done. I use this strategy only for avoided tasks I can complete before the end of that workday. I also contrast how relaxed I'll feel if I get my avoided task done compared to if I've let it slide again.

20. Use What Already Works for You More Often (and Consider Applying It to Other Situations)

Do a tracking experiment for a week or two. When something happens that naturally helps you out of avoidance, make a note of it. For example, you get a specific type of supportive comment. It boosts your mood to the point you're able to start an activity you've been avoiding. In this scenario, you'd note what the comment was and incorporate the same message into your self-talk.

By doing a tracking experiment, you'll probably become aware of strategies you naturally use and the skills and social resources you already have available for helping you break through procrastination. For example, you might notice that when you feel avoidant, you talk tasks over with your spouse to think through the steps you need to take.

In most cases, it's easier to increase a strategy that you already use than it is to begin using a whole new strategy. Now that you've read through most of this list of strategies, it'll be easier for you to recognize what tactics you currently use successfully and increase your use of those.

Especially look for how you can employ strategies you successfully use in one life domain in other life domains. For example, strategies you use effectively at work that you could apply to managing avoided aspects of your personal finances.

21. Get Mere Presence Support

Mere presence support is when you ask someone to hang out with you while you do something you've been avoiding, such as cleaning out your garage or running errands. The person doesn't help you; they're just there for company.

TRY AN ANTI-AVOIDANCE PROJECT

People usually have themes to their avoidance and procrastinate doing specific tasks related to that theme. Let's say you're intimidated by technology. You find yourself getting frustrated very quickly when you're unsure how to complete an action with one of your devices or when you're required to use unfamiliar technology at work. You either ask for help immediately or put whatever needs to be done into your "too-hard basket" and hope for the best.

Using technology-related tasks as the example, part of the problem in this sphere is that you likely have a "you don't know what you don't know" problem. You don't know which technology skills and behaviors you could easily master that would dramatically improve your technology experience. For example, installing an ad blocker on your laptop's web browser might turn out to be incredibly simple but very satisfying, except you don't know that.

Find someone who is skilled in the area of your avoidance who could give you a list of meaningful actions you could try related to your avoidance theme. For example, going through all the menus under Settings in your phone and exploring what's there. or searching for an answer to one of your technology-related questions on YouTube.

Once you've accumulated a list of behaviors you think would be worth doing, assign each suggested behavior a number from 0 to 10 to indicate how challenging you'd find that behavior. Then work through them from easiest to hardest.

There is a wide variety of choices for themes you could target for an overcoming avoidance project, depending on what you avoid. For example, you could try asking a very assertive (but non-jerk) friend, colleague, or family member what sorts of assertiveness behaviors they'd recommend you try, such as calling to request a fee waiver or making a special request at a restaurant. For some themes you can probably come up with a list on your own. For example, if you tend to avoid expressing your warm emotions and positive thoughts, you could make that the theme. You might experiment with expressing love, admiration, respect, gratitude, and enjoyment. You could target verbal, written, and physical expressions of emotion.

If you tend to hoard, you could make throwing stuff away your theme. Work up from the items you'd find easiest to discard to what you think you'd find harder but clearly should throw out. Other themes are avoidance related to money, delegating, and prioritizing. If you tend to avoid relaxing, you could even pick pleasure as the theme. As in the other examples, you'd start with whatever you'd find easiest and work your way up.

Extension Experiment

If avoidance is a major issue for you, you may want to go back through the list of strategies and note a specific example for how you could use each strategy for your currently avoided tasks. The operative word is *could*. You don't need to commit to doing it. The idea is to brainstorm, relate the material to your life, and get to the contemplation stage of change.[7] Doing this will obviously take a while. For many people, avoidance is their most detrimental pattern of self-sabotage. If this is you, you may want to make this chapter your main focus for action.

Still Feeling Really Stuck?

If everything you've read here still feels too hard, you may be suffering from some form of depression. This is particularly true if chapter 4 (on pleasure and self-care) also felt very difficult for you. Heavy-duty avoidance and anhedonia (an inability to feel pleasure) are both classic signs of depression. It would be self-sabotaging to use unguided self-help alone if you have a major clinical problem. If you think you might be depressed, your best option is likely to seek treatment. You can still incorporate self-help (including this book), but do it alongside professional treatment for the specific clinical problem you have.

Moving On

Try answering these questions before moving on to the next chapter.

❏ What's your existing number one strategy for overcoming avoidance? Which strategies from this chapter are you already good at?

❏ Which strategy from the list are you most interested in trying?

❏ What are 1–3 themes of your avoidance?

PART 3

Thinking Blind Spots

CHAPTER 7

. . . .

Spotting Thinking Errors—Part I

There are a huge range of thinking traps people routinely fall into. Over the next two chapters, we'll dive into some of the key patterns that set people up for failure. For the most part, we're all prone to these biases, and they affect us across all life domains. You can't permanently inoculate yourself against these thinking errors. Instead, I'll show you how to recognize when you're making them and then fine-tune your thinking as necessary.

Seemingly Minor Decisions

A pattern known as the *apparently irrelevant decision* is *almost the definition of self-sabotage*.[1] The term refers to seemingly innocuous choices that send people down the path of getting derailed from their intended behavior. Let's run through some common scenarios. You'll notice that even though the term used for this concept is *apparently irrelevant decisions*, the decisions are obviously not irrelevant when you shine a spotlight on them. I personally prefer the term *seemingly minor decisions*, and that's how I will refer to them for the rest of the chapter. If the term doesn't gel for you, you might need to find another term that works for you and helps cement the concept in your head.

To illustrate the concept, here are some examples of seemingly minor decisions (or SMDs):

You have a habit of running late. It causes conflict in your relationships. You have to go somewhere important but you attempt to do "just one more thing" before leaving the house, invariably making you late. You make the decision to do the extra task, even though you know it will create a problem.

You have an important project you're working on. Instead of just sticking at it, you opt to start another project, even though you know deep down that any energy you devote to the new endeavor will reduce the time you have for your existing project and decrease your likelihood of success.

You're cutting back on spending but decide to go check out the Black Friday sales "just to look." Or you sign up to an email list or download an app that will alert you to sales at a particular store.

You're trying to bicker less with your partner. You casually bring up a topic you know tends to lead to conflict, when it wasn't necessary to bring up the topic at all.

A piece of equipment you need for keeping up a good habit dies. You delay making a decision about replacing it while you're debating whether to get the same model or a different one, thus sacrificing the good habit.

You think, I'll just check email quickly before I get started on my high priority work. There are all sorts of scenarios where we think, "I'll just do . . . ," knowing from experience that we're opening ourselves up to the rest of the day getting hijacked. For example, you check work email on the weekend and end up dealing with a work problem after hours.

You buy junk food—not for now, but just to keep it in the house even though you don't need it.

You put your medication away in a cupboard where it's out of sight, out of mind, rather than keeping it where you see it every morning.

Experiment

Understanding your SMDs involves learning which choices change the probability you'll do other behaviors. This sounds awfully technical but it's not such a hard concept once you get your head around it. What do you do that makes doing undesirable behaviors more likely or desired behaviors less likely?

Here are some specific questions you can ask to understand how particular decisions affect your subsequent behaviors, future stress levels, and results. Try drawing a basic flowchart for any situations you can relate to.

Which behaviors affect your mood and then have an impact on your choices? For example: You watch political content at night. → It leaves you feeling depressed. → When you feel depressed, it's harder to take yourself off to bed, so you stay up late, which leaves you tired the next day.

What causes you to get behind at work, not get a lunch break, or go home late? For example, you might have observed that starting a new task within thirty minutes of when you're supposed to leave work results in leaving late 50 percent of the time.

On the flip side, what behaviors increase your chances of staying on track with your day? (We already touched on this topic briefly back in chapter 4, when we covered forms of self-care you skip when you're busy and under pressure.)

When does a behavior subtly set you up for either future stress or future calm? A huge one for me personally is keeping my phone charged. If I keep it juiced, I have it available when I need it. If I think, I'll plug it in later, but don't, I set myself up for stress.

Which SMDs lead to increased future demands on your time? For example, when you invite people to email you, you end up having more email to deal with.

When does not attending to a need right away dramatically increase the time that's required to attend to it later? For example, substances that become sticky if you don't clean up straight away.

How does what you do first thing in the morning affect how the rest of your day goes?

Which very small behaviors have an important impact on your subsequent behavior? For example, If I'm writing and close the document (the microbehavior), I'm unlikely to come back to it that day (a big impact). If I'm planning to take a break rather than finish for the day, I need to keep the document open. This sounds like a tiny insight but it's been hugely important for my productivity. Find similar insights for yourself.

Some SMDs involve behaviors that won't necessarily derail you but increase that possibility. For example, attempting to sneak into the room to grab something while my baby is asleep causes her to wake up around 20 percent of the time. However, because there's no impact the other 80 percent of the time, it's easy to overlook the self-sabotaging effect. When does your behavior only sometimes have a derailing effect but that's still significant?

Solutions

Know your patterns and problem solve. For example, if you've got a tendency to try to squeeze in one more thing before leaving the house, allow an extra fifteen minutes to get anywhere. Set this as your rule of thumb when calculating when you need to leave.

Once you recognize you've made a seemingly minor decision, be prepared to walk back that decision. For example, if you've done a couple of days' work on a project you shouldn't have started, stop working on it and refocus on your most important goal.

Keep an eye out for decisions that make undesirable choices easier or more convenient, or good choices harder or less convenient—for example, you move a piece of exercise equipment to a different room and it becomes out of sight, out of mind.[2]

Try making a time-limited commitment. For example, if you've been bickering with your spouse about politics, commit to a two-week hiatus from talking about that topic. You wouldn't necessarily even need to mention this to your spouse. You could decide and follow through independently of their behavior. If they or someone else raised the topic, you could gently divert the conversation as soon as possible.

Devise alternative plans when needed. For example, if when you host a party you tend to overeat leftovers, your plan A might be to offer the leftovers to your guests. What's your plan B if they decline?

You can choose to think about seemingly minor decisions from the perspective of either what sets you up for failure or what sets you up for success. Do whichever is easier and more fruitful for you, on a case-by-case basis. For example, on the nights you go to bed on time and get enough sleep, what were you doing at 5:00, 7:00, and 9:00 that evening? How did those earlier behaviors make it more probable that you'd go to bed early? You might identify a pattern such as this: If you get your kids in the bath by 7 P.M., 80 percent of the time you end up going to bed on time yourself. You can then work backward to figure out what needs to happen for bath time to occur on schedule.

Understand how subtle aspects of how you think either spur you in helpful ways or stunt you. For example, if I'm writing an article and I think, "Are these points the most important things I've got to say on this topic?" that's a lot more likely to help me produce good work than if I think, "I hope my editor is going to like this," which just results in anxiety. Choose how you think depending on what's most helpful in the specific situation.

The Problem with Should, Must, Always, and Never

Founding father of cognitive therapy Albert Ellis observed in the 1950s that self-inflicted rules that lead to procrastination and/or distress often involve the words *should, must, always,* or *never.* If you're prone to taking excessive responsibility and/or have very high self-standards, you're more likely to get caught in this pattern. For example:

> I must always work harder on a team project than any of my team members.

> I must be good at everything I try, right from the start.

> I must not make mistakes.

> I must keep all my commitments, no matter what.

These beliefs go hand in hand with catastrophizing because, when you adopt this mindset, anything that goes wrong is a catastrophe.

Even if you're not consciously aware of your thoughts, your background thinking processes may be evident from your behavior. If you keep 100 percent of your commitments and backing out of one would seem like a major personal failure, then you probably have an implicit rule that you *must* keep all your commitments.

Here's the problem with rigid rules that, on the surface, might merely seem like having desirably high standards. If the rules you make for yourself are too daunting, you'll likely start to opt out of certain activities because sticking to your self-prescribed standards is excessively hard. For example, you'd like to host a party, but you have a rule: "If I host a party, it must be so good that everyone thinks it's the most impressive party they've been to all year" or "I must make all the food from scratch, and I could never ask my guests to bring anything." When you have these types of lofty self-expectations, your rule makes the prospect of the party overwhelming, so you don't do it and miss out on that experience.

Thinking errors involving should, must, always, and never are common in people experiencing depression or anxiety. When people are in these states, their thinking tends to become less flexible. It's a vicious circle: If your style of thinking is rigid or perfectionistic, you'll be more vulnerable to developing mental health difficulties, and then being in those states will make your already exacting thinking even more so.

There are also versions of these thoughts in which the gist is that other people should always behave competently and do what you want and that events should always go the way you want them to. For example, you think that if you're trying to change lanes on the highway, other people *should* let you in, and it's morally imperative that they do. This type of thinking tends to lead to unnecessary distress because it creates entitlement and low frustration tolerance. People who are prone to blaming others and take little responsibility are more likely to have this version of should/must thinking.

Solution

Try replacing *should* and *must* with *could* or *prefer*, such as, "If I were hosting a party I *could* make all the food from scratch" or "I would *prefer* to keep my commitments, rather than reschedule or inconvenience others."[3] Changing your language slightly opens a crack of flexibility in your thinking. This tiny adjustment can help you see that what seems like a hard-and-fast rule may have some exceptions and nuances.

Experiment

Write out a few statements containing *should*, *must*, *always*, or *never*. Replace the first two words with *could* or *prefer*. Soften or eliminate the latter two words. There's no exact formula. As long as you end up with a more flexible sounding sentence, you're doing it right. Instead of saying, "I must always work harder than my teammates," you might say, "I *could* work harder."

If it's too difficult to think of examples that apply to your life, you can always work through some hypotheticals for now. Doing this will strengthen your understanding of the concepts we've covered. Your own scenarios may come to mind later. Remember, if anything I suggest sounds too hard for right now, identify a version that feels achievable and do that.

Justifying, Excusing, and Blaming

As noted in chapter 2, while some folks tend to take excessive responsibility, other people get very entrenched in patterns of blaming other people or circumstances and justify opting out of anything difficult or uncomfortable. In reality, even people who most of the time take too much responsibility likely sometimes justify, excuse, and blame.

Let's look at some specific examples. I've included the general principle that underlies each example in parentheses. If this topic interests you, check out Gretchen Rubin's series on "loophole spotting."[4]

I can't _____ because _____

I can't exercise this week because I'm on a deadline at work. Or, I can't go for my after-work walk because I've got houseguests. (I can't do X because of Y. They're incompatible.)

I can't figure out how to program my irrigation clock. It's too difficult for me. I'll have to get someone else to do it. (I'm not good at something.)

I can't stop myself from overeating when there's birthday cake at work. Free food is irresistible to me. (I've got no control.)

I can't do any useful work today because I spent forty minutes on hold on the phone attempting to sort out a problem and now I'm tired and in a bad mood. (Blaming circumstances, mood.)

I can't do my fair share of the housework because my spouse is too picky and criticizes me. (Blaming others.)

I can't go to a night class because my kids like me to be home in the evening. (Blaming others, but related to not upsetting or inconveniencing them.)

I can _____ because _____

I can overspend because my spouse overspent on something last week. (Blaming others.)

I can overeat because I'm pregnant. (Blaming physical state.)

I can do X because I'm stressed out and I deserve it. (Blaming circumstances, mood.)

I need to keep ice cream in the house for my kids. I couldn't deprive them of ice cream. (Blaming others, but related to not upsetting or inconveniencing them.)

Solutions

For most people, mixing and matching a combination of the following two options will be required. See what you think.

Option 1: It can be very difficult to sift out valid excuses from flimsy ones. Which justifications are reasonable? When does blaming others or circumstances have an element of truth? If someone has a long commute and argues they're too tired to exercise after getting home from work, isn't that real?

Here's my proposed solution for this. If you have a pattern of making excuses, it's the pattern that's the problem. Ignore the validity of specific excuses and justifications. This is a radical concept that can be hugely powerful. For example, you think, "I didn't do X because my spouse didn't remind me." Is this a valid excuse or not? It may or may not be in any particular circumstance. Under this strategy that doesn't matter. Instead, ask yourself, "Is this way of thinking harming me? Is it harming my relationships? What impact does this thinking have on my behavior?" Try caring about whether a thought is helpful, more than whether it's true.[5] Shift your thinking in ways that help you, realistically, enact whatever behavior is in your own interest.

Helpful ways of thinking involve being *super* kind to yourself and acknowledging your emotions and desires, while still expecting yourself to make the best overall decisions. For example, you're trying to get some recent weight gain turned around, and you find yourself thinking, "I can buy myself a treat today because [name of partner/spouse] bought doughnuts yesterday." Ask yourself whether that's a helpful way to think, rather than whether it's a valid way to think. Alternative self-talk might be something like, "I could buy myself a treat. It's understandable to feel envious and want a treat when someone else is indulging. I certainly deserve to have things I enjoy. However, I've got choices here."

There's no foolproof algorithm for finding self-talk that works for you. It's part science and part art. Research confirms that self-compassion is effective for promoting good decision making.[6] The art component involves blending self-kindness and self-responsibility in a way that feels authentic and meaningful to you. Experiment and see which types of self-talk lead you to the best choices.

Option 2: In some situations, you can test a thought.[7] For example, you think, "I can't get work done because my day has been disrupted and now I'm in a bad mood." I can relate to that pattern of thinking, but I'm often surprised about how productive I end up being on days when I thought that feeling sluggish or grumpy was going to get in the way of my creativity or concentration. It might take me fifteen minutes or so to get into the groove of working, but it just takes a little longer rather than being impossible. If I commit to showing up at my computer and get started, I can get into (or back into) my flow. Allow yourself to enjoy being pleasantly surprised when you test a thought and surpass your expectations. Show up and see how it goes, without huge expectation.

If you think you're too tired to exercise, take a walk around the block and see what happens. If getting started energizes you, you can always walk farther. If it doesn't, you come home and plop yourself on your couch. You tested the thought, and on this particular occasion, you were too tired. The example of overeating due to pregnancy is also very testable. You could try eating a bit more (instead of a lot more) and see how that goes. If you're hungry an hour after eating two burritos, maybe you do need a third one today.

Experiment

Pick either of the strategies mentioned and write out an example of how you could apply it to one of your recurrent justifications.

Not Seeing All Your Available Choices

We often underestimate the opportunities that are available to us. Your sense of your choices will be, at least somewhat, anchored to:

Your current/past choices.

How you see your personality.

The choices of the other people around you (that is, what other people who are near you, or who are similar to you, typically do).

Let's look at each of these in turn.

Your new choices are anchored to your old choices: If you're an iPhone user and your phone needs to be replaced, you'll usually just buy another iPhone. This approach saves excess decision making. However, there can be times we're overly anchored to decisions we've made in the past. We might overestimate the difficulty of switching our choice or may underestimate or be completely unaware of the benefits of doing so. In chapter 13, which is on self-sabotage related to money, we'll look at how biases like loss aversion and the halo effect can cause our behavior to too closely just follow our past behavior.

Your self-identity limits your choices: You may never consider acting in a way that's inconsistent with your dominant view of yourself. Or you may briefly consider it but quickly rule it out. For example, you might think:

I'm a polite person; I couldn't express my anger.

I'm an easygoing person; I couldn't possibly ask directly for what I want.

I'm a humble person; I couldn't draw attention to my accomplishments.

I'm an authentic/honest person; I couldn't possibly be socially strategic to get what I want in this circumstance.

I'm an emotional person; I couldn't be cold and clinical in my approach to this problem.

No matter the human trait, we all have it, just in larger or smaller amounts. When we rigidly stick to a particular self-identity, it can reduce our behavioral flexibility and sabotage our results. When you see yourself as multifaceted and your nature as nuanced, it makes it easier to behave flexibly without it seeming inauthentic.

Every new situation provides us with an opportunity to bring any side of ourselves we want to that situation. Ideally, you'd choose to bring whatever qualities would be most helpful in that specific instance. However, it often doesn't occur to us to veer away from our most dominant side. For example, you're someone who is very thorough, and it generally serves you well. However, in terms of cleaning up your house you find that when you can't be thorough you avoid doing anything, and it's causing you problems. In what ways is utilizing a good enough approach for getting things done also part of your personality? How could you bring that side of yourself to cleaning up your house?

The effect of other people: Behavior is socially contagious. For example, both men and women are more likely to have a first child in the years after a female sibling gives birth.[8] This makes sense from an evolutionary standpoint, given that an experienced parent is now available to guide the new parent.

The choices the people around us make can limit or expand the options we see ourselves as having. In some cases, we may be completely blind to options we have if we don't know at least one person who has walked that particular path. For example, I recently heard that a female friend was planning on taking a solo two-week trip to India (for pleasure) without her children or husband. I remember thinking, "Wow, as a mother I wouldn't have even considered it a possibility to go on an international vacation by myself."

Solutions

How is your nature more nuanced than you typically notice? Pick an area of your life in which you're currently sabotaging yourself, like the house-cleaning example. What's a nondominant part of your nature you could bring to that situation instead, so your new behavior would still be authentically you? What examples do you have from your past when you displayed that alternative side of yourself to good success? Your examples of exhibiting that alternative side may be in a completely different life domain than your current problem.

Sometimes we need only one role model to show us what's possible. Are there any situations where you'd feel more empowered to make a particular choice if someone in your social circle had done so? Choices like the following:

- Hiring an overseas au pair for child care rather than using day care.
- Taking extended paternity leave.
- Working remotely for a corporation and traveling internationally while still maintaining a 9–5 work schedule in the time zone where the company is headquartered.
- Retiring (very) early.
- Adopting a child.
- Moving somewhere you don't know anyone—for example, a different state or foreign country.
- A long-term relationship between a younger male and an older female.
- Running for elected office.

How could you either connect with someone who has already done whatever you'd like to do or be the example for others? The introvert version of connecting with others might involve things like listening to podcast interviews.

Come up with ways in which your work, hobbies, and interests might provide opportunities to interact with people who think in interesting ways that are perhaps different from your default way of thinking. I tend toward being rule-abiding and emotional/sensitive and find it easier to think small than think big. Therefore, I find it very useful to have people around me who are more analytical, blunt, and big thinking and who have less regard for rules. I like it when other people subtly push me in these directions through their example. Thinking, "How would X think about this?" helps me go beyond my dominant way of thinking.

Experiment

A widely quoted saying from motivational speaker Jim Rohn is, "You are the average of the five people you spend the most time with." Regardless of how strictly true this is, it's an interesting thought experiment to consider what it would indicate about you *if it were true*. Who do you spend the most time with? How do those people influence how you think and act, and specifically, how do those people affect what opportunities you see yourself as having?

Mixing Up Causes and Consequences

In self-sabotage, there are a lot of circular chains, self-fulfilling prophecies, and chicken or egg situations. It can be difficult to sort out causes from consequences.

Here are some common examples in which people typically consider the thinking, feeling, or situational element as the cause and the behavioral element as the consequence:

When I think of a good idea, I'll get started.

When I feel less anxious, I'll take more action.

When I feel more certainty, I'll take more action.

When I have more energy, I'll take more action.

When I feel more connected to my (romantic) partner, I'll behave more lovingly (this is a cycle we'll address in chapter 9).

When I feel more confident, I'll offer my skills and talents to others more.

When I feel better about my body image, I'll start more active hobbies.

When I have more time, I'll take more breaks.

It can be useful to flip these statements and think about them in reverse. For example, when I take more action, I'll feel more certain. When I offer my skills and talents more openly to others, I'll feel more confident. I personally notice that when I take more breaks, I feel like I have more time. If I'm overworking, days pass in a blur. In contrast, taking breaks gives me the sense of time slowing down.

Of course, the distinctions between causes and consequences are often muddy. However, because behavior is more directly controllable than thoughts and feelings, it can be more helpful to think of your behavior as the cause and your thinking and feelings as the consequence.

Whenever you're waiting to act, try flipping your thoughts. For example, your default is, "When I have more experience, I'll think bigger." You could flip this to, "When I think bigger, I'll gain more experience." If you think big, you may start to see ways to gain valuable experience quickly, without exposing yourself to significant downside risk.

Flipping your thought won't always direct you toward the right thing to do, but it will challenge your thinking and help you see the situation from a different perspective.

In relationships, we often think of our behavior as a reaction to other people and wait for others to change before changing ourselves. This can easily create a stalemate and unnecessary ongoing tension. For example:

When my sister antagonizes *me* less, I'll antagonize *her* less.

When my in-laws are more accepting toward *me*, I'll be more accepting of *them*.

Experiment

Try flipping an "I do X because of Y" thought to see if there is value in the reverse perspective. For example, I could flip "I task switch because I'm exhausted" to "I'm exhausted because I do so much task switching." The former is more true, but the latter emphasizes that task switching is exhausting! Another example might be flipping "I overeat because I'm lazy" to "I'm lazy because I overeat." Both versions likely have some truth to them. If you're feeling frumpy and lethargic from overeating, you probably opt out of activities.

Moving On

Try these questions to see how deeply you've processed the material from the chapter.

❏ What's one seemingly minor decision involved in your self-sabotage?

❏ What's one justification that causes problems for you?

❏ What's something you'd like to do but you currently think, "I couldn't possibly...."?

CHAPTER 8

· · · · · · · · · · · · · · · · · · ·

Spotting Thinking Errors—Part II

I n this chapter, we'll continue our look at biases that lead to poor choices and/or distress. We'll move on from talking about thinking distortions related to self-regulation to discussing some more general biases that affect decision making and the life directions people take.

Confirmation Bias

· ·

After you've formed an idea, your brain will tend to grab on to evidence that supports your conclusion, and you'll ignore or minimize other data points.[1] This is known as *confirmation bias*. For example, if you like someone, and they act in a way that's irritating or unscrupulous, you'll tend to give them the benefit of the doubt. In contrast, if you don't like someone, you'll tend to judge their behavior harshly.

There are many other examples of confirmation bias, such as:

A prospective home purchaser who falls in love with a house but then finds it difficult to change their view when the inspection turns up negative results.

A product developer who sees huge potential in an idea but ignores relevant evidence that suggests they should have less optimism (for instance, products similar to their idea have not been popular).

A doctor who comes up with an initial diagnosis but then doesn't give enough consideration to other plausible possibilities.

A scientist (or politician) who ignores or minimizes data that are inconsistent with their theories.

A parent who forms an opinion about their child's personality or about best parenting practices and is then resistant to changing that thinking when other evidence emerges.

Once we've formed an opinion, the ways we behave help sustain our thinking errors. Here's how:

Perhaps the doctor doesn't ask their patient about symptoms that relate to alternative causes and therefore cuts off the possibility of obtaining information that would point to the correct diagnosis.

A scientist who is committed to a theory is likely to collaborate and conference with colleagues who also support that theory.

A parent who believes in a particular parenting philosophy likely selects books and articles that promote that philosophy and friends who hold similar beliefs.

Solutions

The main strategy for minimizing the impact of this bias is to habitually and actively look out for evidence that doesn't support your view and supports another view. For example, if you're a political campaign manager who thinks your candidate is going to win in a landslide, you'd actively look for any signs suggesting otherwise.

To stay open to other possibilities, we need to be aware of when we might form a conclusion too early. Especially at work, policies and procedures are useful for preventing confirmation bias. For example, a doctor shouldn't make a firm diagnosis before they've collected a full history from their patient. If you work in a team, then your team meetings should include some type of mechanism that encourages dissenting opinions. If you work alone, then you need a personal process that helps minimize confirmation bias, such as getting external feedback on your plans from an(other) expert.

As per the last chapter, surround yourself with people whom you see as smart but who think in a fundamentally different way from you.

Recognize the upside of having contact with people who have a "disagreeable" personality, meaning they're naturally inclined to point out problems and take an opposing viewpoint.[2] People who are willing to voice dissenting opinions are valuable. They may not always be the easiest to deal with from an emotional perspective (you can end up with hurt feelings or become frustrated with their lack of enthusiasm), but they can challenge your thinking and prevent you being led astray by confirmation bias. Having disagreeable people around you may be especially valuable if you're in an environment that doesn't encourage original thinking. When creative ideas are supported and free flowing, disagreeable people may become less useful.[3]

One aspect of confirmation bias is that once we establish what we think is the best way to approach life, we stop being open to good ideas that come from people who approach it differently. For example, if you're judgmental of people who live conventional lifestyles or, conversely, of people who make alternative lifestyle choices, you're not going to consider or learn from the upsides of the other approach.

Think about qualities that drive you nuts in other people, yet you can also see how those qualities can be helpful in some respects. There is often (not always) something to learn from what irritates us. For example, I'm strongly drawn to batching tasks. I'd rather spend a full day doing something every three months, than do a little bit each week. I usually see the latter as inefficient. When I'm more open, I can see situations in which I'd be better off changing my strategy.

Notice if you think a particular way because you *want* that to be true or because it conveniences you, rather than because it is necessarily true or the best thing for everyone. For example, you think kids should have screen time so they develop technology skills. However, you think this way because *you* don't want to change your device usage, and you can't keep using devices in front of your children all the time without them wanting to do it too. In cases like this, acknowledge the motivation behind your thinking and take care not to ignore evidence that opposes your view. Doing so will help ensure your decision making is as evidence based as possible.

Experiment

Thinking through the different roles you have in your life (manager, parent, friend, and so on), what are the ways that ignoring evidence could cause significant problems for you? How could you create a process that would prompt you to actively look for evidence that runs counter to your preexisting ideas?

Humans Share Negative Information More Often Than Positive Information (at Least in Some Contexts)

Evolution has set us up so we have a natural tendency to warn others of danger. There's less of an evolutionary reason to share positive information compared to the survival benefits of sharing negative data points. It's more critical to point out poisonous berries than safe ones. Likewise, it's more important to warn others that someone is untrustworthy than to remember to mention how nice someone is. People also share negative word of mouth recommendations as much to benefit themselves as to benefit others. Doing so gives individuals a way to self-validate their experience and resolve any sense of injustice they feel.[4]

In modern life, the reality of this bias is that, whenever we google anything, we're more likely to read negative information than positive. You therefore get a skewed picture of reality. If you're anxious or tend to over-research, this can be distressing and/or paralyzing. When you're trying to avoid a bad decision, it can be very difficult to make a purchase or even to decide to try a new restaurant, because it can seem like every option has bad reviews.

There are many scenarios in which this distorted picture of reality is likely to cause unnecessary anxiety. I remember during my pregnancy that my anxiety about labor was heightened because so many of the labor stories I read online were negative. A similar scenario affects people who are managing chronic pain or ill health. People whose treatments are working well for them don't tend to be spending all day on internet forums telling people that. It's the people who are struggling and who are searching for further answers and support who are going to be more active and sharing their stories. Therefore, if you're googling for personal stories about managing your condition, what you'll read is likely to be skewed to the negative.[5]

Solutions

Use base rates and objective data to make decisions. For example, if you have a condition and 80 percent of people with that condition are helped by a medication, there is a good chance it's going to be helpful for you.

Seek out positive stories to balance out negative information. For example, if your doctor is advising you to take a medication for your bipolar disorder and you're scared to do it, ask them to tell you some anonymized stories of other patients who are doing well on the same medication. Sometimes there are options for seeking out positive stories online. When I was pregnant I came across a website that would connect anxious soon-to-be moms with moms who had had positive labor experiences. I didn't use the service, but just knowing of its existence was reassuring.

When you're perusing reviews, as well as looking at the star ratings, read the text of the reviews to see if the points mentioned are even important to you. For example, if a computer review complains about the lack of a backlit keyboard and you don't use your computer in the dark, then that's not relevant to you. Likewise, if a device has poor battery life but you're never far from an outlet, that's not going to be a problem.

Also when looking at reviews, pay attention to how many there are. For example, if you're researching doctors and there are only a handful of comments compared to the hundreds of people who see that provider every month, the reviews (good or bad) probably give you only very limited info.

When someone shares gossip, ask yourself whether the gossiper is doing it to show off their social knowledge or status within a group. This applies especially when you're new to a workplace and may be being inadvertently co-opted into office politics before you've had a chance to get to know colleagues for yourself and form your own impressions.

Experiment

Can you think of anything in your current life for which other people's negative stories are unjustifiably prominent in your mind? How could you better put the negative information in context so it doesn't adversely affect your behavior or feelings?

We Think What's True for Other People Won't Be True for Us

Ironically, another widespread thinking bias is we tend to think we'll be more rational than other people.[6] We believe we'll be immune from (or at least less vulnerable to) cognitive biases and the behavioral missteps that stem from them. Overall, almost everyone expects to be better than average, especially when it comes to domains we perceive to be important.[7]

Here are some examples. If you recognize yourself and feel embarrassed, know that making these errors doesn't mean you're not smart, nice, or ethical. Take a self-compassionate approach when you become aware of flaws that you share with many other good people.

You think:

You'll be able to remain unbiased in situations in which you have a conflict of interest—for example, a doctor who treats their own family or a politician who stands to personally benefit from law changes they're involved in.

Even if most people who sign up for gym contracts end up hardly ever going to the gym, you'll be in the minority who attend regularly for the entire term of their contract.

Even if most people can't stick to X diet, you'll be able to, despite having tried virtually the same diet previously and not succeeded. In other words, you might think that for other people past behavior is a good predictor of the future, but that's not necessarily true for you.

Even though many people tell you that caring for two kids is more than twice as hard as caring for one child, you're sure it won't be the same for you.

Even if many people tell you that the reality of giving birth didn't end up resembling their birth plan, it will for you. You assume other people weren't as committed to their plan as you are to yours.

Even though many parents and grandparents are biased toward seeing their offspring as more gifted, talented, and unique than they are, your child *really is* much cuter than the average baby.

Even though most people (including you) don't enjoy seeing other people's vacation photos, other people will want to spend thirty minutes looking at yours.

You can drive safely while fatigued (or texting) even if other people can't.

You think you won't be as vulnerable to marketing and other business tactics as other people are. For example, even if using a credit card causes most people to spend more than when they use cash, this won't be true for you.

Making a behavioral commitment won't sway your thinking, even if it sways other people's. You think you'll be likely to cancel subscriptions after the free trial period is over. Or if you buy two items and plan to return one, you'll actually end up doing that rather than keeping both.

Even though you've watched a hundred shows on HGTV that depict how overpersonalizing your decor will make your home harder to sell, *your* personal touches will be appealing to others.

You'll be less likely than the average person to unconsciously racially stereotype other people.

You won't fall into the trap of judging people who are similar to you more positively or of judging very attractive people more positively (as smarter or more benevolent, for example) than less attractive people.

Solutions

As a starting point, assume that what's true for most other people will be true for you. Try to feel positive about the idea that you're like everybody else rather than disappointed you're not more special. A big advantage of being like other people is that all these biases are well studied. Whenever thinking errors are negatively impacting you, you can take simple, practical steps to lessen that impact. For example, in the case of signing up for free trials and then forgetting to cancel, you could institute a personal policy of always buying al-la-carte, rather than getting sucked in to subscriptions or contracts (more on this in chapter 13).

Experiment

To stretch your thinking, identify one additional example of where you think you'll be less vulnerable to a thinking error than the average person is; come up with one that's completely different from the examples on my list. Pick something that, on closer inspection, shows that you're probably more average than you'd like to admit.

HOW *NOT* TO BE A PERSON WHO IGNORES POTENTIALLY SERIOUS HEALTH-RELATED SYMPTOMS

Just as people generally see themselves as less biased than the average person, most people believe bad things will be less likely to happen to them than to the average person.[8] For example, you think you'll be less likely to get cancer, develop a heart problem, or get

burgled than most other people. Because this bias has such potentially dire implications, it's worth some focus.

In this box, I'll provide suggestions for how you can make sure
that if you notice potentially serious health symptoms you don't delay
following up. Let's look at the thinking that causes people to delay
seeking help in this situation.

- When people notice a physical symptom such as a lump, a change
  in their bowel habit, or slight bleeding, they may oscillate between
  thinking "It's probably nothing" and having fleeting intrusions of
  dread, "What if this is something terrible and I'm going to die?" Both
  minimizing the potential danger and catastrophizing can lead to procrastination. Make sure you think about the variety of outcomes that
  fall in between nothing and disaster.

- It's also common for people to think, "I don't have time to deal with
  this right now," "I've got too much going on, I can't deal with another
  thing," or "Everything is going well for me and I don't want to interrupt
  it." In response to this thinking, you might consider that if the
  symptom turns out to be nothing serious there will be very little interruption to your life, but if it is serious then the interruption will be
  worth it to get onto the problem early.

- People sometimes think, "I'll be annoyed if I go to the time and expense of a doctor's appointment and then my problem goes away by
  itself next week." In reality, losing a few hours work and being out of
  pocket your insurance co-pay are minimal compared to the potential
  benefits if your problem needs further attention. Perfectionists, who
  need to always get it right, may be particularly vulnerable to this
  thinking.

As previously mentioned, it's paradoxical that people who worry a lot are often the least likely to make concrete, logical plans for dealing with problems because the thought of doing so feels too overwhelming. Having a practical, concrete plan for what you will do if you notice any potentially concerning health changes will help you worry less, and make better decisions.

Solutions

- Know what's normal for your body. For example, if your bowel habit is irregular, such as sometimes constipated and sometimes loose, and it becomes one of those more consistently, then that would be a change in bowel habit for you. Likewise, know what your weight, heart rate, and blood pressure usually are.

- Have a time in your week when you're able to make personal appointments if necessary. For example, you have no work meetings on Wednesday mornings, so if you need to go to an appointment during work hours, this is the best time for you to do it.

- If you see your doctor regularly for a chronic health condition (for example, you go every six months to get a new prescription), set a calendar reminder the night before your visit so you can have a brief think about any change in your symptoms or any new symptoms you've experienced, including anything seemingly unrelated. Write yourself a note, so you'll remember to mention this information at your appointment.

- If you start having any symptom, make a note of the date the first time you notice it. For intermittent symptoms, note whenever you get them. It's easy to underestimate or simply not remember how long a problem has been occurring, For medical professionals to make the best decisions, the patient's account of the history of the problem is often as important as the examination or tests.

- Have a specific list of what symptoms you might experience that would warrant seeing your doctor—for example, headaches if you don't usually get headaches, swollen lymph nodes when you don't have a cold; a change in the appearance of a mole; a change in bowel habit; or any lumps, pain, bleeding, or discharge.

- Use a friend as an accountability partner. Make an agreement with a friend or close work colleague that if you notice any unusual physical symptoms you will tell each other and hold each other accountable for getting checked out promptly.

- Imagine someone else were having the same symptom. If that person were your partner, child, or best friend, would you want them to seek a professional opinion quickly? If you have children, you might think about what you want to role model. How do you hope they will handle the same types of issues when they become adults?

- When you're well, book an appointment with your doctor so you can ask questions you may not have time to ask otherwise, such as about screenings you should have based on your family's history (such as surveillance colonoscopies for bowel cancer).

- If you're married or partnered, ask your spouse to make a doctor's appointment for you if you have thought of or mentioned the need to do this but have not followed through yourself. This isn't to abdicate your self-responsibility, but it's a safety net if you're letting it slide.

- Recognize that we tend to underestimate how well we'll cope when bad things happen. If you end up needing to have further investigations or treatment, you'll likely handle it better and with less disruption to your life, productivity, and creativity than you expect.

Moving On

❏ What are the 1–3 take home messages you'd like to remember from this chapter?

PART 4

Relationships

CHAPTER 9

· ·

Solving Sabotaging Patterns in
Romantic Relationships

The trio of chapters in this part of the book will help you reduce self-sabotage in various kinds of relationships. The first two chapters cover romantic relationships and the third covers friendships and work relationships. There's abundant research evidence that the quality of our bonds with other people is extremely important to our overall life satisfaction, at least for most people.[1] Therefore, we'll give relationships a lot of focus.

The strategies I'll show you in this chapter are aimed at committed, nonabusive couples in long-term relationships (rather than newly dating couples or partnerships in which violence or other major issues are present). I'll show you how to identify and modulate common self-defeating patterns so you can become the happiest you can possibly be in the relationship you're in.

There has been much more research on romantic relationships than on friendships and other types of relationships, which is why books like this tend to have the most to say about romantic relationships. However, as you'll see, many of the broad principles can logically be extrapolated to other relationships such as with siblings, friends, parents, managers, team members, and in-laws.

At first glance it seems that solving self-defeating patterns in romantic relationships should be doubly hard compared to tackling your individual patterns. After all, you're dealing with two people's quirks and emotional baggage. That, however, is not necessarily the case. The patterns that sink couples have been well documented through extensive research studies, and the solutions for avoiding these pitfalls aren't as complicated as you might think. Let's look at some straightforward strategies to prevent a relationship sliding into negativity, or to course-correct if that has already happened.

Reducing Arguments Versus Increasing Your Positive Bond

When couples are arguing frequently, they tend to overfocus on reducing their arguments and overlook opportunities to increase their positive bond. Research has shown there's a surprisingly simple formula that predicts whether a couple will be generally happy or unhappy: To sustain relationship contentment, partners need to have at least five positive interactions for every one negative exchange. When couples are close to divorcing, they tend to have around a 1:1 ratio of positive to negative interactions.[2]

Couples who are stuck in a pattern of frequent arguments tend to overlook the importance of increasing their positive exchanges. They may instinctively know that positive interactions are key to closeness but feel overwhelmed about how to do that successfully anymore or disinclined to want to. A related scenario is when a couple isn't arguing frequently but are drifting apart. They also need to increase their positive exchanges to strengthen their bond.

The reason improving a positive bond needs to come before a focus on reducing arguments is that, if you don't have a positive bond, you won't have much spirit of cooperation. To care about someone else in the midst of an argument, you need to activate your sense of positive attachment to that person.[3] The psychological thorn is that you won't feel like being warm and loving with your partner when your positive bond is low. If you wait until you feel like it, your relationship will go further downhill. Instead you have to act loving to feel more loving. *Actions first.* When you lead with action, the change in your thoughts and emotions will happen automatically.

It's normal for long-term relationships to go through patches of negativity or for partners to feel disengaged during prolonged periods of stress. The tiniest bit of action can change the trajectory of your emotions so that your downward relationship spiral turns upward. Once you've got a more positive bond, you'll find yourselves arguing in healthier ways. Let's take a peek at some flowcharts that show how these spirals play out.

Here's a flowchart of the negative spiral.

Couple's positive bond is low.

⬇

They don't feel like being warm and loving.

⬇

They withhold warm and loving behaviors.

⬇

Positive bond between them weakens and deteriorates.

⬇

Arguments increase.

⬇

Cooperative spirit for managing arguments and reconnecting is low.

⬇

Arguments become more destructive.

Here's the positive spiral.

Couple act positively toward each other, even though
not feeling like it initially.

⬇

They start to feel more loving.

⬇

Even if they argue, the emotional tone of the
arguments improves and they make more effort to repair
the relationship after destructive behaviors.

⬇

Bond improves.

When you're out of the habit of having positive interactions, it can be difficult to even think of ideas for how to have one. Perhaps everything you think of feels too hard with whatever amount of goodwill you're currently feeling toward your partner. To get you started, let's run through some very simple and quick ideas now.

Experiment: Micro-Action Plan

In this section you'll find a big list of micro-actions for increasing your positive bond. Many of the ideas take under thirty seconds and will deliver outsize benefits for the time invested. Grab your highlighter. As you read, mark the ideas you're most interested in. As usual, I'm giving you lots of selections so you can choose what most appeals. Consider doing this experiment as a project by trying one suggestion per day over the next few weeks. You don't need to try everything, but for this experiment in particular, consider going outside your comfort zone a little more than you usually would. Being willing to go outside your comfort zone with your partner helps build emotional closeness and trust. When a suggestion doesn't appeal or doesn't fit with your circumstances, *retain the principle* and adapt the specific suggestion to better suit your situation and preferences.

Note: Some of these may sound corny! Recall how easy it is to react dismissively to ideas that seem simple. Complex, elaborate actions aren't necessarily more effective than easy ones. And, as I mentioned, you can always adapt the ideas or just use them as a springboard for your own ideas.

1.   Call your partner by an affectionate nickname. Try one you haven't used before or resurrect a blast from the past nickname you've almost forgotten about.

2.   Try mental time travel. Mention a good memory of something you did together in the recent past. For example, "I really enjoyed when we sang in the car together last week." Savoring positive emotions is an effective strategy for increasing happiness, especially when you savor your milder, everyday type emotions.[4]

3.   Make a positive comment about one of your partner's friends. It doesn't need to be over the top. For example, you could say "Your friend X is really good at calling you when you haven't seen each other in a while." Why is this tip effective? It says:

   I'm tuned in to your life.

   I understand what you get out of being friends with that person.

   I don't think all the judgments/choices you make in your life are completely nuts.

4.   Make a loving comment in support of your partner about something that's stressing them out. This helps cultivate compassion.

5. Tell your partner a short joke. Act like you're having fun telling it. Savor the telling of the joke and their reaction. Telling and understanding jokes is fun, absorbing, and a little bit challenging for your brain, so it also takes your mind off stress. It's a win–win. You can always google a joke if you can't think of any.

6. Show appreciation for a job your partner does. Say thank you to your partner for a job they do that benefits you both, but that you rarely spontaneously thank them for.

7. Give your partner a thirty-second shoulder rub. The reasoning behind this tip is the same as why newborns are placed on their mom's bare chest straight after birth. Physical touch, especially if it's skin to skin, activates the bonding hormone oxytocin.

8. Express admiration for some aspect of your partner's character that they have self-doubt about.

9. Tell your partner about the last time you were pleased you took their advice. This is the principle of allowing mutual influence (more on this later in the chapter).

10. Give your partner a six-second hug. This releases oxytocin and serotonin (natural, feel-good, bonding chemicals).[5] Concentrate on enjoying the sensations of the hug.

11. When you reunite with your partner at the end of the day, make the first thing you say be about something that went right for you during the day. For example, "My meeting with X went really well. Better than I hoped." Research has shown that sharing positive news and experiences benefits both the sharer and the recipient, and strengthens the relationship between the two people.[6]

12. Have a moment of loving eye contact and smiling at each other.

13. Mention something you like about how your partner expresses love for you. (*Note:* This shouldn't be a request or a complaint in disguise. Cite a behavior that your partner already does freely.) For example:

    I love it when you tell me what a good singer I am.

    I love it when you call me [insert affectionate nickname].

    I love it when you grab me and kiss me.

14. Sing a few bars of a song to your partner while making eye contact. Choose a song that has a romantic connotation, such as "How Sweet It Is (to Be Loved by You)."

15. Mention looking forward to something you will be doing together in the near future. For example, "I'm looking forward to hanging out on the couch together on Friday night." This is a variation on the mental time travel concept mentioned in micro-action 2. That version involved reminiscing about a positive event from the past. This version is about looking forward to an upcoming activity.

16. Make a positive comment about a personality trait or habit that your partner shares with their parent(s). For example, "I love how X you are. I can see you got that from your mom." Or "I love how X you are. I can see you learned that from growing up in your family." If referencing their parent doesn't fit with your partner's family situation, you could substitute any person who has been a mentor in your partner's life.

17. Mention a way your partner has positively influenced you. It could be as simple as an interest or hobby that your partner introduced you to. Or it could be some way your thoughts have

shifted due to your partner. (Again, more on this strategy coming up.)

18. Tell your partner something you're embarrassed about but logically know you shouldn't be. Rationale: Sharing soft emotions and vulnerability allows your partner an opportunity to get emotionally close to you.

19. Increase your nonverbal expression of positive emotion. For example, give your partner an extra big smile in reaction to something sweet or cute they do. Displaying positive emotion with your body is likely to intensify your experience of that emotion, so this strategy benefits the giver and receiver.

20. Acknowledge a good point your partner has made when you have been discussing one of your recurring areas of tension or disagreement. Do this for a point you don't typically acknowledge. For example, "You're right I forget things less when I write them down. It's a good idea."

21. Express support for something that is going right for your partner at the moment. For example, "I'm so pleased your blog is doing well. I'm really happy you're having success. You deserve it with how hard you've worked." This is an especially important mini tip if *you're* socially anxious. Supporting people when things go right is known as providing *capitalization support*, and this tends to be a weakness for people who are anxiety prone.[7]

Variations: If you want to make this micro-actions experiment more spontaneous, you can put each of the suggestions on a piece of paper or card, place them in a bowl, and draw one per day. If your partner is onboard, you can do the experiment in "two-player" mode and each draw a suggestion per day. Don't tell each other what you drew until after you've done the associated action (for example, wait until the next day). For anyone who wants to try it this way, I've made a template of the twenty-one micro-actions that you can easily print out and cut up. To download it, see http://healthymindtoolkit.com/resources.

Growing as a Person through Your Relationship

This section will be useful for either staying on the right track in your relationship or getting back on course if the positives you get from being in your relationship have waned over time. To feel fulfilled in a relationship you should have an ongoing sense that you're growing as a person through your partner. There will be ebbs and flows, and this sense won't be totally constant, but it should be mostly there.

At the start of relationships, growing via the partnership happens easily. We get exposed to new interests and habits when we become involved with a new partner, and our self expands as we incorporate some of our partner's likes, thinking, and ways of doing things into our own repertoire. This growth could be from your partner introducing you to a great cuisine or TV show, a new circle of friends, a different perspective on a political issue, or an easier/better way to do a task. New partners also help us see positive qualities in ourselves that we previously may have been blind to.[8] For example, you may not have realized that your sense of humor was so positive and desirable until your new partner helped you see that. This is how relationships can help us improve our self-esteem.

When you know your partner very well, your sense of growth can stall. If your relationship starts to feel stale, you may need to give it a deliberate kick start to reinvigorate a sense in both of you of growing from your being together. Here are ideas for doing that.

Grow Your Intimacy through Deep and Meaningful Self-Disclosure

Experiment

If you've been in a relationship for years you might think you know everything there is to know about your partner. Discover some corners of your partner's thoughts you haven't explored before. To do this, try Professor Arthur Aron's thirty-six questions. Art is one of the founding fathers of relationship science. The questions come from a study about how mutual vulnerability leads to love.[9] The questions start out relatively low key and get increasingly more personal. You can access the questions via *The New York Times*; google "NYT 36 questions" to find them.

Other simpler variations:

Ask your partner's opinion on a topic for which you don't know their thoughts in much detail, perhaps a political issue. Pick a topic where you're genuinely interested in allowing your own opinion to be influenced by your partner's ideas.

Ask a question about your partner's childhood, such as, "Tell me about what you loved to do during summers as a child." Use your judgment in what you ask. Don't pick questions you think will trigger arguments.

Turn Your Tension into an Opportunity for Growing Together

Healthy relationships involve both partners allowing the other person to influence their thoughts and actions. This shows trust and respect. This can be challenging in areas of tension, but here's how you can do it.

Experiment

Try one of the following suggestions.

What's a quality your partner has, or a behavior your partner does, that both irritates you and that you secretly admire in some respects? For example, if your partner is very easygoing they may not worry when they're going to be late for events. If you're always hurrying them up in a stressed-out way, at some point mention (without snark) that, on some level, you admire that they're so relaxed about being late. You don't have to love their relaxed attitude to time in all respects to acknowledge the positives you see.

Ask for your partner's advice in an area that, at least tangentially, relates to a topic of tension. For example, if your partner is always nagging you to tidy up, ask their advice about some aspect of organizing. Pick a question that you expect your partner will be surprised and delighted you asked. This suggestion, and the previous one, can also be especially useful for improving other types of relationships in which you have tension, such as with your in-laws.

Proactively bring up a topic your partner has wanted and attempted to discuss but you keep fending off or shutting down the conversation. For example, if your partner has been nudging you about whether you want to have another baby, you might say, "You've been right that we need to talk about that. Want to talk about it tonight on our walk?" You don't have to come to a consensus but at least your partner will feel heard, the conversation will bring you closer, and you will likely make some progress toward coming to a mutual decision.

Perspective Taking: The Multi-Tool of Good Relationships

I'm not going to focus much on reducing arguments, but I will mention a particular skill that can work almost like magic for dissolving relationship tension. *Perspective taking* is an extremely useful (and simple) relationship technique that has an incredibly wide range of uses. We often *think* we've considered our partner's perspective, but in truth, we haven't really done so in any detail. Partly this is due to the *false consensus effect*, whereby we assume others see the world the same way we do.[10] (In fact couples who've been together a long time may be the ones who are most likely to fail to do accurate perspective taking and empathizing.[11]

Perspective taking can help you see another person's emotions and reactions as reasonable rather than bonkers. It can also often help you recognize your own biases in how you're viewing a situation. For example, whether you're seeing your partner's behavior through the lens of entitlement or another bias, such as "My partner should do the dishes straight after dinner because that's the way I think it should be."

Do brief perspective taking whenever you have a sense of friction in your relationship. For example, you're frustrated with your partner's avoidance behavior and therefore you are nagging them every day. However, you've not considered how it feels to be on the other end of that nagging. Or you're frustrated with how your partner acts with their parents. They procrastinate telling their parents about decisions they've made because historically their parents have had huge negative overreactions to their life choices. You've never really imagined how hard it is for your partner to tell their parents stuff, always expecting a rejecting reaction.

When you've imagined your partner's perspective in detail, you'll tend to naturally choose more effective behaviors for attempting to influence them and/or be more accepting and understanding about their actions.

Experiment

Pick an issue about which you're feeling frustrated, disappointed, or angry with respect to your partner's behavior. Try perspective taking in three steps.[12] Describe the situation from your own point of view. Next, describe the situation from your partner's point of view. Third, describe the situation as a neutral observer might view it. Ideally do this by writing three short paragraphs rather than just thinking it through.

Here are a few extra tips for perspective taking:

Often it's useful to check the accuracy of your perspective taking. Say to your partner, "This is what I'm imagining this situation is like from your point of view. Am I on the right track? Am I missing anything?"

Some people find that getting visual distance helps them get more psychological distance and makes perspective taking easier. To do this, imagine you're looking down on whatever situation is bothering you from the upper corner of the room (where a security camera would be mounted). Use perspective taking as a check on your own actions. Ask yourself, "Would I act this way with other people?" For example, you might walk in the door from work or errands without greeting your partner, but you probably wouldn't do that to anyone else.

Perspective taking can instantly dissolve relationship tension or frustration, even when those emotions have been present for a while and you feel very annoyed. Use your emotions (annoyed, frustrated, etc.) as a cue to try perspective taking.

The tips we've covered in this chapter apply to virtually any couple. In the next chapter, we'll look at how individuals' attachment styles impact their relationship patterns, strengths, and vulnerabilities and what to do about it.

Moving On
. . . .

Try these questions to check how deeply you've processed the material in this chapter. If you can answer these questions relatively easily, you're ready to move on.

❏ What strengths of your relationship did this chapter highlight? Name three positive, relationship-enhancing behaviors mentioned in the chapter that you and your partner already do routinely?

❏ Was there anything mentioned in the chapter that you hadn't previously recognized as a strength of your relationship but you now see as important? For example, you ask each other's opinion regularly and you hadn't realized what a strength of your relationship that is.

❏ What's your highest priority area for improvement? What's your partner's highest priority?

CHAPTER 10

· ·

How Decoding Attachment Styles Can Help You Understand Yourself, Your Partner, and Other People

It's not smart to negotiate with people you love as if you were conducting business transactions. What generally matters most in relationships is emotional trust. This gets undermined by score counting—that is, when partners attempt to negotiate "I'll do X, if you do Y," and then keep track of who is best keeping up their end of the bargain. There's no one-size-fits-all solution for achieving emotional trust. To have the best shot at it, you need to understand both your own and your partner's *attachment style*. Attachment style is what we'll cover in this chapter.

Therapists classify a person's attachment style as being either secure or one of several different types of insecure styles. Having an insecure style isn't rare. Around 50 percent of individuals have an insecure style, meaning that there's a good chance that one or both partners in any relationship will be insecurely attached.[1] Once you understand how attachment styles work, you'll know how to decode your own and others' behavior and how to bypass barriers to closeness and trust.

This chapter is focused on romantic relationships. Most people have the same attachment style across different relationship types. In the next chapter we'll unpack how attachment styles play out in friendships and work relationships.

> ## IMPORTANT!
>
> Although having insecure attachment style sounds like a negative, it doesn't need to be. People with secure styles typically have an easier time in relationships. However, just like there are advantages and disadvantages to being an optimist versus being a pessimist (or an introvert instead of an extrovert), people with insecure attachment styles have strengths too. We'll cover the strengths and weaknesses of each style.

When you're attempting to understand your own or your partner's attachment style, take care not to fall into gender stereotyping. You may have to look past stereotypes of needy females and aloof guys to accurately understand your partner. For both men and women, the most common attachment style is secure. Likewise, there are plenty of men with anxious styles and women with avoidant styles.

Overview of Attachment Styles

What's Your Style? (And Your Partner's, If Applicable)

Read the descriptions in this section to identify your attachment style. As with anything related to personality, every individual will have a dominant style but may not fit 100 percent neatly into one of the boxes. Identify both your dominant style and any aspects of the other styles you have. You can also take an attachment style quiz by researcher Chris Fraley available at http://www.web-research-design.net/cgi-bin/crq/crq.pl.

Very long term research studies that have followed individuals from infancy to adulthood have shown that people generally keep the same attachment style as they age (but relationships can influence this).[2] The parenting a child receives and the child's temperament play roles in what attachment style the child develops, as does the fit between a parent's nature and their child's nature.

Because insecure attachment styles are so common, it wouldn't be reasonable to conclude that only horrible parents produce children with insecure styles. Also, one set of parents often produce children with different attachment styles. It may be just a slight mismatch between the child's emotional needs and the parenting they receive (magnified over time), combined with the child's temperament, that produces an insecure style.

Although there is a degree of consistency in someone's attachment style over their lifespan, it's not set in stone either. When attachment style does change, it's usually in predictable ways that relate to the person's life events (more on this later in the chapter).[3]

Note: The names traditionally used to describe the three attachment styles are secure, anxious, and avoidant. However, having an anxious or avoidant attachment style isn't quite the same as being anxious or avoidant in general. There's overlap but they don't map one to one. For example, someone who has an anxiety disorder might have an avoidant attachment style. *In this chapter only, when I refer to avoidant or anxious people, I'm referring to attachment style, not the general tendencies.* I'm using the terms researchers have given the concepts, even though it is a bit confusing. I apologize in advance.

The Securely Attached Person
Someone who is securely attached likely grew up with parents who accurately and promptly responded to their emotional needs. They typically see themselves and other people positively. They generally trust other people, and don't expect to be broken up with or otherwise abandoned. They're comfortable relying on others and having others rely on them. Because they feel secure in relationships, they don't feel easily threatened

by their partner's friendships, interfering in-laws, or their partner having time-consuming interests that don't include them.[4]

Securely attached folks are generally good at paying attention to their partner's emotional reactions, meaning they're able to read their partner's emotions accurately and, in turn, respond helpfully. They can usually tolerate *some* insecure behavior (such as their partner acting needy or withdrawing) without it freaking them out.

If secure people have a weakness it's that they may not always understand what it's like to feel insecure, and therefore they may not totally get why someone who is insecure can't just suck it up and act more secure.

The Anxiously Attached Person

This characterization of someone with an anxious style will sound on the extreme side. If you have this style, you won't have all these features, and many of the features you do have may emerge only when you're feeling insecure. If you notice yourself or your partner in the description, it's not your cue to panic or be critical. All of the sabotaging patterns mentioned here can be easily avoided using straightforward skills and strategies, as you'll see by the end of the chapter. In fact, *I* have an anxious attachment style, but because I follow the same tips I'm sharing here, it doesn't cause major problems for me.

Someone who is anxiously attached typically grew up in a household in which they were given the message (perhaps subtly) that their emotional needs were overwhelming to other people. Their parents may have either responded inconsistently or misread their emotions. Anxiously attached babies tend to be very distressed when briefly left alone with a stranger, but then display anger when their parent returns, whereas in the same scenario, securely attached babies are easily comforted when their parent returns. As adults, anxiously attached folks tend to alternate between idealizing their partners and being angry at them. They can be very demanding and needy when they're not feeling secure. They get caught in a self-fulfilling prophecy where the more they worry that their emotional needs will overwhelm others, the more insecure they feel, and the more demanding their behavior gets. The more intense they get, the more likely it is that others will, in reality, find their behavior overwhelming and either withdraw or leave.

The strengths of people with anxious attachment styles are that they're typically very loving, want to bond closely, and think about their partner a lot, including keeping their partner in mind when not physically together. An alternative term for an anxious attachment style is *preoccupied*. Folks with an anxious attachment style are emotionally full on. They feel both love and hurt strongly.

Although they're very loving, anxiously attached people can get caught up in their own feelings of being in love rather than their feelings being truly about their specific partner. They can be self-absorbed in taking care of their own intense feelings and not pay close attention to their partner's emotions and reactions. This can lead to being erratic. They may alternate between acting loving and engaged when they feel like it and ignoring their partner or behaving less responsively at other times. When someone pulls away from them, they chase. When someone meets them emotionally, they may freak out and back off. Alternatively, they may feel bored by the lack of emotional intensity they feel when they're not chasing someone's love.

ANXIOUS ATTACHMENT STYLE: SABOTAGING BEHAVIORS AND THINKING PATTERNS

Here's a quick cheat sheet of the sabotaging patterns associated with an anxious attachment style.

People with an anxious style will often:

- Pick arguments with their partner during times of personal stress, instead of using the relationship as a source of comfort.

- React with anger when a separation is coming up—for example, pick an argument when their partner is about to go on a business trip—or when reunited after a separation.

- Push their partner's emotional buttons as a way of getting a reaction, especially if they sense their partner is withdrawing from them. They may act needy or demanding as a way of testing their partner's love and commitment. Any emotional engagement from their partner feels better than no engagement.

- Think and feel like they're giving more to their relationship than they're getting back. This arises from their tendency to be very intense. They may think of their partner as selfish and self-centered because of their own high expectations. When their level of intensity isn't returned, they may feel disappointed and develop the idea that relationships will always fall short of expectations. They may idealize their partner at first and then become disenchanted.

- Compartmentalize their relationships. Compartmentalizing makes an anxiously attached person feel less emotionally vulnerable. They might talk to particular friends (or their parents) about certain problems but don't share these problems with their partner. This is a way of guarding against having all their attachment eggs in one basket, which, given their relationship insecurity, feels very threatening to them.

- Reignite arguments once a discussion has moved to neutral topics, instead of using those discussions as a chance to cool tension.[5]

The Avoidantly Attached Person

People who grow up to have an avoidant attachment style were typically somewhat expected to look after their own emotional needs as a child. They may have spent a lot of time playing by themselves, and perhaps had parents who worked a lot (through necessity or choice). They've usually experienced caregiving that was rejecting or dismissing. For example, LGBTQ individuals who are rejected by their family or when someone who experiences abuse is not believed or protected by the adults around them. Around 25 percent of people have an avoidant style so it's not just the most extreme cases of rejecting caregiving that result in children having this style, and once again, the child's temperament plays a role in what style they develop.

The strengths of people with avoidant attachment styles are that they're self-reliant and low maintenance. On the surface, people with avoidant attachment styles are very good at tolerating separations. However, in reality it may be that they don't recognize the effect that separations have on them. For example, in studies of babies, those with avoidant styles showed little external reaction when their mother left the room. However, by measuring the infants' heart rates, researchers showed that the children found being separated from their mother physiologically stressful.[6]

Avoidantly attached people may not have a lot of faith in others being able to soothe them or help them processes their emotions. Avoidant individuals' typical MO is just to withdraw when they're feeling stressed or when they need to cool off after a relationship argument. Avoidant people will typically react very badly if their partner acts anxious or needy. They have no tolerance for that behavior. For example, they may become mean or mocking in response to anxious or needy behavior because it feels so intrusive to them. If two avoidant people are in a relationship, they can seem more like ships passing in the night than a tightly connected team. Because neither partner is naturally inclined to chase or to stay emotionally connected while working out difficult problems, relationships in which both people are avoidant are at higher risk of failing.[7]

Avoidantly attached folks are inclined to say things like, "I'd be fine without you" or will unfavorably compare their current partner to a past partner, without recognizing how hurtful or rejecting those types of comments can be. They may have a clinical or practical approach to relationships, such as seeing the relationship as a convenient way of getting regular sex or household help.

Researchers sometimes break down avoidant attachment into two styles, known as *fearful avoidant* and *dismissive avoidant*.[8] Those who are fearful avoidant will have a low opinion of themselves and may avoid dating. They're typically doubtful about the potential for finding lasting love. As intimacy or commitment increases in a new relationship, their MO is often to nitpick a partner's flaws as an excuse to leave a relationship, rather than deal with the increasing emotional entanglement of a longer-term relationship.

Those who are dismissive avoidant will have a high opinion of themselves. They may have serial relationships, bailing on the relationship if their partner attempts to get them to commit. People with a dismissive avoidant style may fail to be warm and welcoming when reuniting with their partner after a period of separation. For example, I recall seeing what appeared to be a dad being picked up at the airport by his partner and small children. The dad barely acknowledged his family, wheeling his bag in front, with his family trailing behind, and he completely missed the looks on his kids' faces indicating that they needed a hug and kiss hello.

Individuals with a dismissive avoidant style can be confident and charming. They may show intermittent flashes of being emotionally responsive, loving, and caring, but lack consistency. If you're in love with someone with a dismissive style, you probably love them for something other than being consistently responsive. For example, you admire their out-of-the-box thinking, their risk taking, or their business acumen and vision. When the relationship is going well, you may think of their flashes of emotional responsiveness as their real self. When the relationship isn't going well, you may find yourself thinking that their cold and callous side is their real self. However, more realistically, both of these sides are part of who they are.

Various cleverly designed research studies have shown that avoidantly attached people want to feel bonded and close to other people, even if they don't always recognize this themselves.[9] For example, just like everyone else, they experience increased positive mood and greater self-esteem when they're told (in the process of participating in a research study) that they're accepted by others and that they'll be successful interpersonally in the future.[10]

AVOIDANT ATTACHMENT STYLE: SABOTAGING BEHAVIORS AND THINKING PATTERNS

Here's a quick reference guide to the sabotaging patterns associated with an avoidant attachment style.

- Whereas anxiously attached people push their partner's buttons to get their partner's attention, avoidantly attached people may push their partner's buttons as a way of pushing that person away so they can get some emotional distance.

- Avoidantly attached people tend to withdraw emotionally during times of personal stress rather than use their relationship as a source of comfort.

- Avoidantly attached people may leave their partner feeling left out and not notice when their partner feels hurt by that. For example, they greet their kids when they walk in the door in the evening but don't greet their partner.

- They keep parts of themselves separate from their partner and attempt to process their emotions on their own, rather than fully letting their partner into their emotional world. This can lead to misunderstandings when they fail to communicate their thoughts and emotions to their partner.

- They may react angrily and dismissively if their partner wants attention when they want space to be alone.

- Their avoidance of letting people into their emotional world creates a self-fulfilling prophecy by which their expectation that other people aren't a useful emotional resource gets confirmed by default.

Creating and Maintaining Healthy Attachment Bonds and Emotional Trust with an Insecure Attachment Style

How can a couple create and maintain healthy attachment bonds and emotional trust, even if one or both partners have an insecure attachment style? I've heard psychology colleagues flippantly say that if you want to have the easiest possible time in your relationships, you should pick partners (and friends) who are securely attached. While this is somewhat true, life doesn't always work out so conveniently. If you love the person you're with, you can learn to appreciate aspects of their attachment style and see their strengths. We all have our own wiring, baggage, and emotional intimacy preferences. When someone who has an insecure style feels secure in a particular relationship, their underlying insecurity may be barely noticeable. And when a person with an insecure style achieves emotional trust in a relationship, their general style will gradually shift to being more secure over time.

Develop Habits That Don't Leave an Avoidant Person Feeling Intruded Upon or an Anxious Person Feeling Unanchored

There's a concept in relationships psychology called the *magic five hours*.[11] According to this theory, it takes only five hours per week to keep your relationship on the right track. This time is made up of mindful hellos and good-byes (such as when leaving for work and arriving home); a twenty-minute de-stressing conversation each day, expressing affection and either admiration or appreciation daily; and a block of two hours of alone time as a couple once a week (for example, a date night).

Part of the beauty of this formula is it helps people of various types meet their attachment needs. If you make a habit of having a stress-reducing conversation for ten to twenty minutes or so each day, that's going to help an avoidant partner not feel excessively intruded upon, and it's going to help an anxious partner not feel ignored. Likewise, if you're expressing admiration and affection (even in a very small way) on a daily basis, even the most anxious partner is going to be getting plenty of messages that the relationship is secure.

Manage Personal Stress Effectively

Anxiously attached people need to manage their tendency to pick arguments when they're under personal stress, such as after experiencing frustrations at work. Picking arguments because you're feeling pressured or frustrated causes additional stress, creates a less harmonious home environment (which might result in your kids acting up), and makes your partner feel less inclined to want to support you. It takes trust but, if possible, allow your partner to call you on picking arguments due to personal stress when they notice you're doing it. Your partner needs to be able to say things like, "You're lashing out at me because you're disappointed about what happened at work today" and have you acknowledge when that's true or slightly true.

If you have an avoidant style and want to process your feelings alone, find ways of communicating that need in a way that doesn't leave your partner feeling rejected or shut out. There's some evidence that, especially after traumatic experiences, people who have an instinct to process their thoughts and feelings by themselves, without discussing them, should be allowed to do that.[12] Preferring to do this isn't a problem. The only issue is not communicating to your partner that this is what you're doing.

You might say to your partner, "I'm going to go for a run to think about how I should handle [the problem situation]. Once I've done that, maybe we could watch an episode of [a favorite show] together?" Including a statement about wanting to be together after you've had your alone time is important. Say it, rather than assume it doesn't need saying. If you don't want to talk about your thoughts and feelings but *would* like another type of emotional comfort, ask explicitly for what you *do* want from your partner: "I've had a rough day. I don't want to talk about it, but I could use a long hug."

If you like to have some alone time after work, expect to need to interact with your family at least briefly before you get that alone time. For example, spend fifteen minutes with your family before you go out and tend to the garden by yourself. They love you, and if they haven't seen you all day, they'll want to connect with you. Figure out a strategy that meets your needs and theirs.

Share Your Positive Thoughts and Emotions

If you're someone who prefers not to talk out your stress, pay extra attention to the role of sharing your positive experiences for sustaining your emotional connections with other people. Tell your partner about what you have coming up that you're looking forward to. If you've been at work or running a long series of errands, you can share what has gone well for you on your outing or that you're pleased to be back home with your family.

Extra tip: If you *must* express a negative when you first see your partner after a separation, then try expressing sadness or disappointment rather than anger or frustration, where applicable. For example, if you're feeling peeved because you went out to buy an item and it was out stock you might lead with, "Well, that was disappointing, they were all out" rather than expressing your anger or frustration. Why do this? Expressing soft emotions (the type that people don't express with clenched fists) activates caring and attachment behaviors in other people, whereas expressing "fighting" emotions doesn't usually evoke caring reactions in others. If you're excessively negative (for instance, you're constantly expressing your sadness, anxiety, loneliness, or disappointment), then your partner may start to react with anger to those emotions rather than support.

Understand How Attachment Fears Play Out in Your Relationship

In his book *Wired for Love*, Stan Tatkin points out the core fears that people with insecure attachment styles are typically prone to. People who have an avoidant style usually fear feeling intruded upon, feeling trapped or out of control, too much intimacy, and being blamed. In contrast, people who are anxiously attached fear abandonment, separation, being alone too long, and that their emotions are burdensome or overwhelming to other people. If you have an anxious or avoidant style, one or two of these fears may be the most prominent for you.

A useful way to think of these fears is that no one likes to have these feelings (that is, no one likes to feel blamed, trapped, or intruded on). The discomfort of experiencing the emotions themselves is relatable to everyone, regardless of attachment style. However, people with insecure styles have a lower threshold for these particular fears being triggered and a more intense reaction when they are.

If one or both of you is insecurely attached, get to know how the fears mentioned in this chapter play out in your relationship. For example, if your partner has an avoidant style, you may notice that they react as if they're being blamed even when you're not blaming them or when you're blaming them a little but not in a way you see as a big deal. If someone is still talking about how they're not to blame half an hour after a minor incident, there's a good chance that person has an avoidant attachment style.

Here's an example that relates to an anxious style. Someone who is anxiously attached will often need reassurance that their partner *wants* to be there for them emotionally. Try saying to an anxious partner something along the lines of, "I love that we get to come home to each other after stressful days." Or "I love that whenever we're dealing with the ups and downs of life, we're doing it together." A person with an anxious style is likely to feel deeply soothed when their partner references the relationship as being a tight team, as in, "This situation with X is difficult, but we're a team and we'll get through it together."

When either partner is insecurely attached, both partners need to look out for attachment-related fears showing up in the relationship, *without blaming or shaming*. For example, both people can be alert for when an avoidant partner is reacting to feeling trapped or when an anxiously attached person picks an argument before a separation. You'll need to find a way to let each other know when you've spotted something, in a way that won't get the other person's back up. There's initially an element of threading a needle to this, but once it becomes a normal part of how you communicate with each other, it'll get much easier.

Find Small Tweaks That Make a Big Difference

When it comes to soothing attachment fears (or making sure they're not activated in the first place), it may be only small tweaks that are needed for both people to feel good. For example, asking, "When would be a good time to talk about X?" rather than launching directly into the conversation may be enough to stop an avoidant person from feeling hounded.

If you can be very clear about what you need to feel loved and secure, it can keep a lid on intense emotions and prevent either person from feeling overwhelmed. For example, if you have an anxious style and are concerned about your partner becoming tired of you expressing your thoughts and feelings, you might communicate that your emotional needs aren't boundless by saying, "When I'm feeling stressed about a personal issue I need to tell you about it for five to ten minutes." Chances are that both people will feel better after a short debrief rather than a sixty-minute marathon. An excessively long conversation potentially gives the anxious person more time to get wound up and go around in circles, while the person on the receiving end becomes increasingly drained and annoyed.

Become Chief Expert at Pushing Your Partner's *Positive* Emotional Buttons

If you have an insecure style, coping with your own emotions can get in the way of paying close attention to your partner, including noticing what activates their pleasurable emotions. To each get better at this, observe what your partner's face and body look like when they're feeling different types of pleasant states, such as pride, joy, excitement, or relaxation. If you're good at triggering some pleasant emotions in your partner but not other types, try triggering the ignored emotions. If you're uncomfortable soothing someone's distress, you can gain confidence by getting better at triggering their pleasant emotions first.

Maintain Healthy Boundaries in Your Friendships and Family Relationships

Improving relationship boundaries can make people with insecure styles feel more secure.

People with anxious styles often feel threatened if specific types of closeness are shared between their partner and other people, but are lacking in their own romantic relationship. For example when their partner seems to enjoy having silly fun with their friends but at home acts serious all the time. Your partner needs and deserves an all-access pass to your positive emotions. Don't save your fun side for your friends and have your romantic relationship be just about parenting and running a household, for example.

There shouldn't be things you tell your friends or family that you don't tell your partner. If you have news, tell your partner first. If you intend to discuss important plans or decisions with other people (for example, you want to run a decision by your parents), give your partner a heads-up that you're going to be doing that, rather than let them overhear you having the conversation without warning. A child's tightest bond is with their parents (in most cases). When you're an adult who's in a marriage or marriage-like relationship, you transition to your tightest bond being with your partner. Parents shouldn't intrude on that bond too much when it comes to big decisions, like where you live, how you parent, whether you switch jobs, or how you decorate your home.

If some of your friends and family don't like your partner, your partner may need reassurance that any opinions those people hold don't impact the security of your relationship.

Be aware of outside hobbies or work commitments that are so absorbing you don't make space for each other.

If you have a busy life, distinguish between family time and couple time. It's easy to have the perception of giving time and energy to your family but overlook that you're directing that mainly to your children.

Read Your Partner's Requests for Attention

Get familiar with the types of circumstances that cause you to ignore your partner's requests for attention. Make an "if, then" plan to help you become more responsive. For example, you might know that you tend to ignore your partner when they try to bring up decisions that need to made about your home or about spending money. Your plan could be, "*If*

I don't have the mental space to have the conversation straight away, *then* I can say that but plan a firm time for committing to a course of action."

If you realize you've ignored your partner's attempts to get your attention, apologize. For example, "I could tell that you were signaling to me that you were tired and wanted to leave the party. I ignored you because I wanted to stay. I'm sorry for ignoring you and not considering that you needed to get to bed so you'd feel refreshed for work." When you act in ways that are inaccessible or unresponsive in a relationship, the process of genuinely apologizing and repairing the breach will deepen your trust and create more secure attachment (providing you don't overuse the apology card).

Learn to Manage Periods of Being Apart

Any parent knows that having a brief break from your children intensifies your feelings of love for them. Adult attachment works the same way. If you have an anxious style, recognize that periods of separation can make your partner feel more love for you. As previously mentioned, if you have an anxious style, you'll probably need to watch out for your tendency to pick arguments before and after separations, or when a temporary separation is being contemplated (as when your partner is talking about going away for the weekend with their friends).

Try being mindful of when you have an urge to nag, nitpick, complain, and so on because you're feeling anxious about an impending or proposed separation. Consider whether overall it's better to not say whatever is on the tip of your tongue. Again recognize, "Oh, that's just my attachment style kicking in," if you find yourself easily irritated when a separation is looming or has just occurred. If your partner has an anxious style, understand that their expressing anger or irritability after a separation is likely driven by their attachment style, and you'll need to do a small amount of extra soothing to help them know you're pleased to be reunited.

If you have an avoidant style, you may need to take steps to minimize how much separations unconsciously affect you. For example, if you've been away on a business trip for a few days, you may need to build in a transition to help you not feel intruded upon when you get home. If you've been on a long flight, maybe you decompress in an airline lounge for thirty minutes before your partner picks you up from the airport. Find what works for you, so you can be emotionally and physically available to your family when you reunite. Your fear of feeling blamed may also get triggered by separations. Distinguish between when your partner is expressing sadness or anxiety over a separation and when they are blaming you when, for example, you need to travel for work.

Understand Which Types of Support People with Different Attachment Styles Prefer

Forget anything you think you know about women wanting listening and emotional support and men preferring problem-solving help when they're distressed. Support preferences are more about attachment style than gender. In general, people who have secure or anxious attachment styles tend to prefer receiving emotional support over practical (problem-solving) help. According to the most current research, people with avoidant attachment styles are different and a bit complicated.

Avoidantly attached individuals typically respond better to practical support (such as problem-solving suggestions). However, their preferences are more nuanced than that. A well-conducted set of studies showed that people with an avoidant attachment style don't respond well to mild to moderate intensity support attempts from their partners.[13] In fact, the studies showed that they responded to mild or moderate intensity practical support by feeling increasingly distressed; perceiving their partner as controlling, critical, and distancing; and feeling less of a sense of self command. However, when their partners provided high-intensity practical support, the reverse pattern happened. The highly avoidant participants felt less distress and greater self-command and became less likely to see their partner as controlling, critical, or distant. Note, the difference between mild, moderate, and high levels of support was in the degree of support and not a difference in specific behaviors, beyond the general categories of practical versus emotional. High-intensity support was that which trained coders rated as at least a 6 on a 1–7 scale of intensity.

Why does such a pattern happen for people with an avoidant style? Receiving low- or medium-intensity support is more ambiguous. At that level, the avoidant person's attachment fears are activated but not adequately soothed. With high-intensity practical support, their deep-down attachment fears are overcome so they're able to benefit from receiving support. Therefore, the general take-home message is that if you're the partner of someone with an avoidant style, you need to go big with your support attempt and keep the support focused on problem-solving rather than emotions.

Understand the Best Ways to Influence Your Partner

If you're attempting to get someone who has an avoidant style to change something about themselves, emphasize their autonomy, validate their viewpoint, and acknowledge their constructive efforts and good qualities. You need to use strategies that don't activate their sense of being intruded on, and that's why emphasizing autonomy is important.[14]

If you're attempting to change an anxiously attached partner, try emphasizing how committed you are to the relationship and how strong the relationship is. For example, "We're great at working together in X respect, I'd like to be as good at working together when it comes to Y."

Understand How Partners' Attachment Styles Affect Each Other

To round out our coverage of attachment in romantic relationships, let's briefly look at how each person's style will impact their partner's. Being in a relationship in which you generally feel secure will make you more secure over time, although it typically won't change your style completely. If you have an anxious style, having an avoidant partner will usually bring out your attachment anxiety more than if your partner wasn't avoidant. On the flip side, if your partner has an anxious style, their anxiety may bring out your avoidance. Sometimes people who are anxiously attached become more avoidant over time if they're with an avoidant partner, through a cycle known as *protest, despair, detach*. When people express attachment anxiety and those feelings are not soothed by an attachment figure (whether that's a parent or a partner), they may eventually give up and become more avoidant.

Both of you should attempt to spot any ways one of you is bringing out insecurity in the other person and use the strategies from this chapter to turn that around. On a positive note, as you try the solutions we've discussed, pay attention to how doing so creates greater attachment security in your relationship. Using the strategies from this chapter will raise the threshold for the types of situations and behavior you can each tolerate without it triggering attachment insecurity. For example, notice if when your partner feels more secure, they're less envious of your friendships with others.

Moving On

Try answering these questions before moving on to the next chapter.

❏ What's your dominant attachment style? What aspects of the other styles can you also relate to?

❏ If you currently have a partner, what's their style? Looking back at your past relationships, what attachment style do you think your past partners had?

❏ Regardless of what your style is, which of the strategies for creating healthy attachment bonds are already a strength for you? Where can you see room for improvement?

CHAPTER 11

....

Friendships, Work Relationships, and Attachment Style

Now that you understand the basic concepts behind attachment style, let's unpack how the two types of insecure styles manifest in friendship and work relationships (for example, colleagues and teams). This chapter is brief because it builds on the previous chapter.

There's been much less research on how attachment styles play out in friendships and at work compared to the thousands of studies on romantic relationships. Therefore, a lot of what's in this chapter I've extrapolated from what we know from research on couples and parents–children rather than from specific studies of friendships or workplaces.

Studies on Friendships and Attachment Style

....

Many of the existing studies on the role of attachment style in friendships have focused on adolescent friendships. And most of what we know is about differences between secure and insecure individuals generally, rather than specifically about each of the insecure styles. Here's some of what we do know from studies on friendships: People who are securely attached tend to have more positive friendship expectations and experiences generally.[1] Securely attached people are more active in using pro-social strategies to maintain their friendships,[2] self-disclose more,[3] and have less conflict in their friendships.[4] There's some evidence that emotionally charged friendship conflicts have a particularly adverse impact on people who have an anxious style and are associated with future increases in depression.[5] Finally, people with avoidant styles tend to show weaker communication skills and poorer focus during problem-solving discussions with friends.[6]

Studies on Work and Attachment Style

In terms of work-specific studies, we know the following: People with anxious styles are unsurprisingly the most anxious about their work performance and relationships at work. People with avoidant styles are prone to overworking.[7] Securely attached people are more confident in their effectiveness in teams and are more likely to be perceived by others as emerging leaders.[8] They also display more vigor and "organizational citizenship behaviors" at work.[9] People with secure styles are less vulnerable to burnout compared to people with either type of insecure style.[10] People with anxious styles tend to prefer external contracts rather than internal, permanent contracts,[11] presumably because these activate their attachment anxiety less.

In the leadership domain, leaders with anxious styles tend to be rated by their followers as being less effective, whereas leaders with avoidant styles are rated as lacking emotions skills.[12] Securely attached leaders are the most likely to delegate, whereas avoidant leaders are the least.[13] People who are managed by insecurely attached leaders are more vulnerable to burnout and low job satisfaction,[14] and groups managed by avoidant leaders are rated as less cohesive.[15] People with anxious styles show the strongest preference for relationship-focused leadership.[16] Finally, people with avoidant styles tend to have lower quality relationships with their supervisors.[17] How attachment style relates to transformational, visionary leadership (if it does at all) isn't clear at this stage.

All this sounds negative if you happen to have an insecure style. However, it's likely that we don't yet understand the circumstances in which insecure styles are beneficial. From an evolutionary perspective, the most useful attachment style to have depends on the context. For example, if you've been abandoned, then an avoidant style helps you emotionally move on and get on with the business of surviving. There are some initial hints about the usefulness of insecure styles at work in studies. One showed that people who have an anxious style are more effective at alerting others to threats when doing so involves acting quickly and bypassing obstacles.[18]

What More Can We Deduce? What Are the Practical Takeaways?

Now let's go beyond individual studies and look at what we'd expect the links to be between attachment and friendships/work relationships based on what we know about attachment overall. Once again, these are generalizations and somewhat extreme characterizations. If you happen to recognize yourself quite strongly in the descriptions, there's no need to feel embarrassed. When you understand your attachment style, the solutions for managing it are quite logical and straightforward, as you'll see when you read the solutions. If you have a secure style, these descriptions and tips will help you understand other people.

Anxious Attachment in Friendships and Work Relationships

Anxiously attached people will likely tend to form intense friendships. As in romantic relationships, they will typically feel worried about friends "breaking up" with them. However, they may run hot and cold on their friends. When they're feeling stressed or distressed, they may seek out a lot of contact with their friends but then withdraw at other times, such as when they're having a friendship infatuation with a new person.

Anxiously attached folks have high expectations that other people will invest the same emotional intensity into relationships they do. This commonly leads to feeling disappointed and angry when this doesn't happen. When they sense a friend is withdrawing emotionally (even if this is due to something totally reasonable like a new job or a new baby), they may become subtly more demanding of their friend. On the flip side, when someone seems to be becoming more intensely interested in them as a friend, they may pull back themselves.

People who are anxiously attached may tend to compartmentalize their friendships—for instance, they may prefer not to share friends with their partner. This is self-protective because sharing friends feels inherently threatening to them. They don't trust their partner not to leave them (or not to gossip about them behind their back) and don't want to lose their friends if this happens.

Because anxiously attached people form intense bonds quickly, they'll often feel closer to others than others do to them. They may form intense attachments to people they know only through the internet or may feel a strong sense of attachment to semipublic people they don't know personally (authors, bloggers, podcast hosts). Internet fan communities (such as those based on being a fan of a specific TV show) may be particularly attractive to people who have an anxious style. These communities provide emotional intensity, a common language to facilitate bonding, and friendship compartmentalization. However, as in other relationships, the anxiously attached person may end up feeling disappointed or let down by these relationships.

In the workplace, people who are anxiously attached are likely to seek out intense relationships with a few specific colleagues. They may feel apprehensive about approaching people at work whom they don't know well. They may believe it's important to be good friends with someone with whom they have a close working relationship. For example, they may desire quite a lot of personal self-disclosure in their work relationships because that type of intimacy helps them feel more secure.

Anxiously attached people will likely find transitions difficult in work relationships, such as when a boss leaves and is replaced. They'll likely feel angry when they have a sense of being withdrawn from, even when this isn't 100 percent logical. For example, if someone they're close to at work starts working on a team project that doesn't include them. They may know that their reaction is out of proportion to the situation; however, logically knowing that won't necessarily soothe their emotions completely.

Solutions

You're practically an expert on attachment style now, so if these solutions seem self-evident, you'll know you've gained a good understanding from your reading. Try whichever solutions relate to how attachment insecurity shows itself in your life.

> Recognize when you're reacting in a way that's out of proportion to the objective situation. If you can be accepting of the emotions you're having and see that it's just your attachment insecurity getting activated, strong feelings can be easier to cope with. For example, if you find yourself feeling angry, upset, or jealous when

a work colleague transfers to another team and it activates a sense of abandonment for you. Or when a friend withdraws from you during a period of change in their life.

If you tend to feel strongly attached to friends or work-mates, recognize that this is your style, and that it has plusses and minuses. If other people don't feel similarly strongly attached to you, that's not an indictment of you as a person. Because you lean toward intense attachments, most other people you meet are going to be naturally less intense than you are.

Try accepting that it's normal to have inequality in how connected you feel to a particular friend versus how connected that friend feels to you. For example, if you feel somewhat intensely drawn to someone you only know from online interactions, that's pretty normal. Try to figure out how you can enjoy experiencing strong feelings of connection without those feelings necessarily being reciprocated.

At work if you tend to have just a few close colleagues and mentors, experiment with forming a broader range of relationships, including some that are less intense and that don't involve a lot of personal self-disclosure or that don't involve a sense of being friends as well as colleagues. A lack of personal friendship in a work relationship isn't a sign of threat, even if it might feel that way given your attachment style.

Notice if you tend to alternate between idealizing certain people and feeling disappointed in them. Try to move toward the middle if you find yourself doing this.

Avoidant Attachment in Friendships and Work Relationships

Because avoidantly attached people are at least superficially good at tolerating separations, they may go long stretches without seeing particular friends. They'll tend to let friends contact them, rather than instigating friendship dates or other catch-ups. Even though they want to see their friends, they'll wait on the other person to do the reaching out. They won't chase up a friend if a plan falls through and needs to be remade. Because they fear feeling intruded upon, they'll generally set up their friendships so that their shared activities are casual and not intimate or emotionally intense. Friendships between two avoidant people likely lack much glue to hold the relationship together, if neither person is willing to be the one who chases up the other. As in romantic relationships, people with avoidant styles may underestimate the emotional impact it has on them when their friendships or important work relationships are disrupted, such as when a friend or colleague they're close to gets busy and has less time for them.

People with avoidant styles will typically have a preference for less emotional intimacy in their work relationships. Because work relationships are often like this anyway, the avoidantly attached person's style may not impact their collegial relationships as much as the anxious person's does. Mentoring (or supervising students) may be difficult for people with avoidant styles because these roles involve the mentees relying on the mentor for reassurance that they're progressing and that any mistakes they're making are a normal part of the learning process. The avoidant person may feel annoyed or at sea if work colleagues seem to want emotional support or self-disclosure from them.

The same fears that show up in their romantic relationships—particularly the fear of being blamed or intruded upon—likely show up in their work relationships too, such as the fear of being held responsible if a team project isn't going well. As in their romantic relationships, people who have a dismissive avoidant style likely display flashes of being considerate of others' emotions but lack consistency. They may make hurtful comments without paying attention to their emotional impact, such as when mentoring a student, compare them unfavorably to a past student.

Solutions

Experiment with being more consistent in the contact you have with friends rather than letting long stretches pass without contact.

Be willing to follow up to remake plans with friends when plans fall through.

Both in friendships and at work, notice if you're underestimating the emotional impact of disruptions in or loss of attachment relationships. Use extra self-care when an attachment relationship you've enjoyed has been obstructed, such as if a close colleague moves to another team.

If receiving high-intensity practical support helps you feel secure, put yourself in learning environments in which you're able to receive that. (Recall the study I referenced in the last chapter showing that's the type of support those with an avoidant style typically prefer.)

At work, have some faith in your capacity to serve as an attachment figure for others, without feeling overwhelmed or intruded upon yourself. For example, suppose you are supervising a student who needs emotional support and encouragement. If the student has an anxious style, you can use the tips from the last chapter to help them feel secure, without it feeling excessively burdensome to you. Pay attention to the sections in the previous chapter on the best ways to support and influence others' behavior depending on their attachment style.

Use positive events as a way to bond with work colleagues (for example, send a congratulations email when someone experiences a success).

Apologize rather than avoid if you've made an attachment faux pas (for instance, you forgot to congratulate someone or ignored a request).

Coping with Workplace Drama

Interpersonal drama in the workplace likely impacts both anxious and avoidant people more strongly than those with secure styles. People with avoidant styles are prone to becoming emotionally overloaded and find it difficult to disengage from negative thoughts.[19] For those with anxious styles, workplace drama will activate their relationship concerns. Therefore, it's especially important that people with insecure styles use extra self-care and strategies to cool their emotions when coping with workplace drama (even when they're not directly involved), and that they use support effectively when necessary, such as dealing with situations involving victimization.

Moving On

❑ What's the number one take-home message you want to remember from this chapter?

❏ How do you think your attachment style has shifted over your lifetime? Broadly speaking, can you see how the relationships you've had have impacted this? For example, if you've become more secure as a result of experiencing emotionally trustworthy relationships—whether those are romantic, friendship, or work based. Or if you went through an avoidant spell after being let down by an attachment figure.

PART 5

Work and Money

CHAPTER 12

. . . .

Self-Sabotage at Work

I n this chapter, we'll tackle four specific sabotaging patterns that relate to work, and then look at microhabits that affect work performance.

Imposter Syndrome

. . . .

Imposter syndrome is when, despite your objective accomplishments, you fear being revealed as a fraud. This leads to attempting to fly under the radar and not stick out. You may feel chronic self-doubt or you may alternate between anxiety and confidence. A feature of imposter syndrome is catastrophizing any mistakes or negative feedback. You fear that if one flaw is revealed it's going to be the beginning of the end of your career.

Imposter syndrome can create a self-fulfilling prophecy of under-achievement. Here's how:

> You may hold back from networking, leadership, voicing dissenting thoughts, and anything else that would draw attention to you or open you up for scrutiny. However, in doing so you miss out on opportunities to demonstrate your value.

Imposter syndrome is often accompanied by fear and avoidance of feedback. If you avoid feedback, you lose opportunities to improve. You also lose opportunities to find out when other people think you're doing well.[1]

You may hold back from submitting yourself for awards, scholarships, or other opportunities that would require external evaluation (like submitting your research for publication). If you don't put yourself forward in these ways, you end up with less objective evidence of your capabilities and achievements.

If you are prone to catastrophizing, you may react badly to feedback. Your defensive reaction may itself become the major problem, rather than whatever the feedback was about.

You may aim lower.

You may act extra charming to compensate for your perceived lack of competence. However, if you're praised, you then attribute it to your charm rather than your effectiveness.[2]

You may opt out of anything that you think could put you on the trajectory toward more responsibility and visibility, even if it doesn't immediately do so. You see some degree of putting yourself out there as a slippery slope toward being under constant scrutiny.

You may believe that only extraordinary performance is going to save you from being revealed as a fraud. This can create issues with excessive perfectionism, competitiveness, paralysis, or even envy. As we've covered previously, perfectionism and envy can lead to opting out, such as holding back from collaborations if they trigger your tendency for social comparison.

Solutions

Don't jump to the conclusion that imposter syndrome means there is anything wrong. Think about someone with obsessive compulsive disorder who, despite having washed their hands ten times already, has the sense there are harmful germs remaining on their hands. They equate that they still feel anxious and icky with there still being actual danger. Imposter syndrome is the same. Just because you feel a sense of danger doesn't mean it exists.

Don't perpetually raise your standards. *Clinical perfectionism* is the term used to describe people whose perfectionism causes problems in their life and increases their risk of developing mental health difficulties.[3] When clinical perfectionists achieve their high standards, they tend to react by raising their standards even higher. What happens is that the person expects that achieving their rigorous self-expectations will make them feel better (less anxious, more self-accepting, etc.). When it doesn't, they erroneously conclude that their standards must not have been high enough and bump them up! This creates a cycle of misery. Don't let this be you.

Be aware of any cognitive biases you have in evaluating how competent other people are. This is especially true when you predominantly hear colleagues or leaders talk about their expert area, such as a university professor who teaches a very specific area of knowledge. Remember that people in leadership roles often get to choose what they feel most comfortable and passionate talking about. You're unlikely to see where they have gaps in their knowledge. They're not choosing to talk about those topics.

We tend to assume that whatever we know, other people must know too.[4] Therefore, your areas of expert knowledge will typically seem ordinary to you, but may well seem extraordinary to others. Recognize if you're doing this.

In a similar vein, if you assume other people think the same way you do, you might overlook that your way of thinking is actually a skill. For example, you automatically look for creative solutions whenever you face a roadblock, but you may not realize that many people don't do this.

If you think other people must know more than you, you may hold back from sharing your knowledge, which can lead to being seen as less valuable. Let's say you learn a small tip that's immensely helpful to you. You believe your colleagues might find it useful too, but you think, "They probably know it already" or "What if I share what I've noticed and others are disinterested?" As a solution, try this: If you think there's a 50–50 chance your colleagues will find your tip useful, share what you have to say. Prioritize the potential of getting a good reaction over avoiding any potential for getting a lukewarm response.

A huge light-bulb moment for me personally has been noticing that I need periods of both self-confidence and self-doubt to produce my best work. Both of these emotional states help me in different ways. Sometimes I need confidence to crank out work or take charge of a situation. On the flip side, sometimes I need self-doubt to propel me to examine where I might have blind spots and to motivate the effort involved in correcting these. Because my ultimate aim is to produce work that helps people, I'm willing to experience a mixture of emotions in order to do that.

Understanding that periods of self-doubt are helpful doesn't make them unpainful. Self-doubt still feels like having a Band-Aid ripped off. However, knowing that periods of self-doubt actually help me achieve makes them feel valuable and tolerable.

Stay cool when you receive constructive or critical feedback. I have a larger section on how to do this in my earlier book, *The Anxiety Toolkit*. Here's the short version: If you are prone to panicking in response to corrective feedback, assume that you are probably overestimating how much you need to do to fix the problem. You may find it helpful to have some phrases on hand to communicate your openness to feedback in moments when you're internally freaking out. For example, "Those are interesting points, let me go away and process what you've said."

Circling back to the material on attachment style from chapter 11, if you're prone to anxiety and imposter syndrome at work, it can be immensely helpful to find supervisors and senior colleagues who you're sure recognize your general competence and who can serve as work-related attachment figures for you.

Pay attention to anyone you avoid or feel envious of because they seem (or are) smarter and more accomplished than you. You don't have to be the absolute smartest person on every topic to protect yourself from disaster. Life would be boring if you knew more than every single other person. Your skills don't need to be extraordinary to be valuable.

Imposter syndrome can pop up when you're making leaps to different levels in your career. You may find it helpful to talk to others who have made those same leaps. Ask them what it was like, in terms of both practicalities and their emotions. This doesn't need to be a deep and meaningful conversation. Sometimes it's simply useful to know that someone else became more comfortable over time, or conversely, that they empathize because they still have moments of feeling a sense of imposter syndrome.

Objectively speaking, your best defense against being perceived as being incompetent is to be competent. Evaluate your choices based on whether they will, in reality, improve your competence; you could ask yourself, "Will collaborating with people who are more skilled than I am lead to me becoming more skilled?"

Develop a deep understanding of your strengths, including the role of circumstance, experience, and luck in creating those strengths. For example, I'm a digital native (we had computers at school and at home when I was in kindergarten), but virtually no one older than I am is. I can source and synthesize vast amounts of research very quickly using technology (hello, Google Scholar), whereas this isn't as intuitive for nonnatives. I also have more experience and a deeper knowledge base than most other people in my field who are younger than I am. Because of this, the ways I make sense of what I'm reading and how I put it into context are different from what people who have less overall knowledge can do with the same information. There are things I'm not as good at as some other people in my field, but I also know I have some uncommon strengths, in part simply due to when I was born.

In addition, when you're thinking about your strengths, remember back to chapter 2, where I discussed how our strengths sometimes rise directly out of our weaknesses. Make sure you understand how this is true for you.

Look at your past. If applicable, where did you pick up the idea that there was something wrong with you or that you weren't as smart as is necessary for success? It can be the subtlest things that can lead to imposter syndrome. For example, your parents responded to you getting 96 percent on a test by asking you about the other 4 percent. Perhaps you compared your intelligence unfavorably to a sibling's. Or perhaps people thought you were weird growing up, and you got the message that your only redeeming quality was your intelligence. Therefore you overvalue intelligence and any threat to that (such as making a mistake) feels catastrophic.

When and how did you develop whatever beliefs you have about what's necessary to avoid professional catastrophes? For example, if you believe that it's important to never make mistakes, when is the earliest you can remember thinking like that? You don't need to dwell on these questions for a long time. However, it can be helpful to understand the ways in which your child or young adult mind used its juvenile reasoning powers to try to make sense of the world and your place in it, but reached an erroneous conclusion that you're still carrying with you as an adult.

Experiment
Which of the solutions seem most helpful and relevant to you?

Not Finishing What You Start

When I asked around to find out what people most wanted to see in this chapter, a popular request was for tips relating to "Not finishing what I start." There is nothing magical about the strategies I offer here. Many times problem solving your patterns is more about having clear enough headspace to think of strategies and how you'll implement them rather than the solutions being particularly unicorn-like or ingenious. Consider yourself having outsourced some of that thinking to me!

Solutions

Use a two-pronged approach of (1) figuring out how you can leave tasks unfinished less often and (2) instituting a mechanism to scoop up partially finished tasks and get them done. When possible, prevention is better than cure, so prioritize strategies that prevent the problem from occurring over ones that force you to go back and complete unfinished tasks.

Address the cognitive error of thinking, "I'll get back to that," when, realistically, you know from past experience you won't. If it feels like too much work to finish it now, what are the chances it's going to feel less effortful later? Notice any instances when you're committing this thinking error and try to correct them.

Understand the seemingly minor decisions that lead to you leaving jobs unfinished. What's the context in which you end up starting tasks that later become part of your half-finished pile? You might share my problem of switching tasks when you're exhausted rather than taking a break, only to quickly run out of steam and end up with both your tasks sitting unfinished.

Another example would be starting a task that will take an hour just thirty minutes before you need to pick up your children.

If need be, do last things first to help pace yourself better. Often when your energy is waning the last part of a task feels tedious. For example, I find it helpful to select and upload the photos for blog posts before I start writing. Otherwise, by the time I've done the creative work of writing I don't have the patience or energy for selecting, resizing, and uploading photos. When the nature of the task allows it, using a last-things-first strategy can help you pace yourself better if you tend to underestimate how long an activity will take.

Try having more acceptance that completing the last 10–20 percent of tasks is often hard. At that point you're tired and you're likely to start mentally seeing the task as pretty much done, even if you still have significant work to do. It's natural to find the last little bit a slog! Give yourself some compassion for this.

Use routines to establish the habit of finishing tasks in one go. When you have routines, you can make sure you have ample time and energy at that particular slot in your work week to do your planned task from start to finish.

Just because you started a task doesn't mean it's worth finishing. Apply the same heuristics you use for prioritizing new tasks to finishing your half-done projects. For example, completing un-finished tasks still fits under my $100 rule. If an unfinished activity isn't worth $100, I'm not going to attempt to get to it unless I've done all my $100+ jobs.

It'll come as no surprise that some of the concepts mentioned in chapter 6 (about procrastination and avoidance) are also relevant to finishing tasks. Make sure your self-imposed rules for how you do a task aren't interfering with getting things done. For example, if I attempt to write a blog post with ten points I'm much less likely to finish it than if I start with three or five points in mind. Are some of your rules and standards based in your own head, but there is no external requirement to do it that way?

As a backstop, put time aside for wrapping up partly finished jobs. Think back to chapter 5 about the idea that you have different amounts of cognitive energy available at different times in your day and week. To have enough willpower to revisit half-done tasks, you might need to use a time slot when you have a high level of cognitive energy available.

Finishing partially completed tasks can be boring compared to the allure of starting a new project. Periodically place a moratorium on starting anything new to force yourself to finish what's incomplete. What are you not going to do until you've finished whatever you've left part done?

Compulsively Overworking

This section is aimed at people for whom overworking is a choice: You're someone who feels driven to overwork either because of a sense of mission or because you think of overworking as necessary to prevent personal failure. If this is you, it's worth experimenting to see what happens when you work less. You may find you paradoxically achieve greater productivity when you put in fewer hours. If not, the personal benefits may still outweigh your lower output or you may realize you've been overestimating the need to overwork (for example, your job performance evaluations don't go from good to bad when you dial back).

Solutions

Give yourself the experience of not overworking. If you're in hamster-on-a-wheel mode, you'll need to step off to get clarity. For example, to get some clear headspace, take a day trip to hike in a national or state park, spend a week without using your phone or computer in the evenings, or go away for a weekend without bringing or checking in on work.

On a very microlevel, try taking a few slow breaths and give yourself permission *not* to work on solving whatever problems you're facing and to instead feel calm for five minutes. Most likely there aren't any disasters that are going to befall you in the next five minutes, so give yourself permission to enjoy just being. If you like this approach, you can gradually stretch it out to longer. This strategy is particularly recommended if you feel nagging stress or a constant crushing sense of pressure. People often overwork because their anxiety spikes the moment they stop working. They temporarily resolve that anxiety by jumping to doing more work. However, in the long term this just perpetuates the problem of feeling anxiety when not working. If this is you, it's helpful to practice mindfully pausing.

Listen to what others have been telling you. For example, if your spouse has been mentioning that you're due for a medical checkup or that you seem to be working long hours on something not very lucrative, there may be a useful nugget (or more) of truth in what they're observing. Other people can be particularly helpful in alerting us to the presence of a problem, even if their thoughts about how to solve it are off base (or downright irritating).

If you're overworking, you may be undervaluing the role of breaks in helping produce the best progress on your work. In many cases, it's simply not true that there is a trade-off between taking breaks and optimal output. Strategies like sleeping on a decision or doing activities that allow deliberate mind wandering (showers, exercising, washing the dishes, driving, etc.) allow your brain to synthesize complex strands of thought and weigh options on autopilot. If you tend to be a deep, deliberative thinker you can have the best of both worlds by putting in some conscious thought (your strength) as you work and, if a clear solution hasn't emerged, taking a break and doing an unrelated activity, letting your brain continue its work while you concentrate on something else.[5] Allow your nonconscious mind to work on your problem for you, using the unique strengths of that type of mental processing. You'll be amazed at how often this will result in quickly achieving clarity on the best way forward. No amount of continuing to bang away at work can substitute for this.

Consider the potential benefits of your other interests cross-pollinating your work life. When you're on a single track with your career, a lot of your knowledge is going to be the same as that of others who are also on that track. Having other interests that influence how you think can give you a huge competitive advantage in your work life because you end up with a combination of skills and knowledge that isn't the same as that of every other person in your field. For example, if you play a sport, aspects of the thinking required for that sport may change how you think in your work life. Maybe the sport requires sometimes using your instincts rather than overthinking it. Maybe from your sport you learn how to muster the grit you need to win in the last few minutes of a game. If your work is very analytical, perhaps you'd benefit from a hobby that relies on your intuitive side. If your work involves a lot of intense emotions (such as being a therapist), you might benefit from a hobby that involves being mathematical and emotionless (if you're also drawn to this). How could an outside interest strengthen a different part of your brain and allow you to connect with another aspect of yourself?

Engaging in a hobby or interest after you've done a period of intense working can be a very fruitful strategy for producing creative insights. Your work will still be on your mind enough that you'll make mental connections between your hobby and your work. Here's one of the strategies I use: Late at night, I'll find a podcast I enjoy and choose to listen to whatever episode from the back catalog sounds *least* interesting to me. This helps me get exposed to more thought diversity. And, in a drowsy state, my mind is happy to wander and make creative connections between new and familiar concepts.

Try this thought experiment: If you were going to do extremely little work, say, two hours per day, what would you do? If you were to delegate or outsource almost everything, what would you end up doing yourself?[6] Thinking about the extreme can sometimes help you see options you couldn't previously see and can crystalize what should be a priority.

When a manager, boss, or teammate is expecting you to overwork, it may just be poor perspective taking on their part. Most of us have a natural bias toward underestimating the amount of work other people do and fail to completely recognize what's involved in work done by others. If you're being asked to do an unreasonable amount of work or aspects of your job are excessively disruptive to your life, helping your leader or teammates see your perspective *may* be enough to correct their expectations.

Understand the psychological payoffs that are contributing to you overworking. For example, check if overworking on one set of tasks allows you to avoid other problems that are more anxiety provoking to you. As mentioned in the last chapter, this is frequently seen in people with avoidant attachment styles. Sometimes people who overwork hold it over their romantic partner as a way of feeling superior, as in, "Look at me, I'm working all the time. Therefore, I'm virtuous and you're lazy." If you're prone to imposter syndrome, consider the association between that and overworking. Are you overworking because you think it's the only way to avoid a catastrophe? Do you overwork to excel or avoid mistakes, which will prevent your feelings of imposter syndrome from being triggered or your (imagined) imposter status from being revealed?

Look to people in your field (those who do the same job at other companies) and/or people with the same family situation as you have who don't overwork. Find out what they do (and don't do). How do they balance work and home? What skills do they have that would help you work less?

Check if you have any faulty heuristics that may be contributing to you overworking. For example, you have this heuristic: If you can do a task twice as fast as someone else, you'll do it yourself. This seems reasonable on the surface, but in reality it might lead to you taking on too much responsibility and keep you from delegating. At the same time, your co-workers or team members will not gain the skills that would lead to their becoming more efficient.

Is the *sunk costs error* causing you to overwork when it's not objectively worth it? For instance, do you persist in trying to correct a problem because of the time and effort you've already spent, when realistically it would be better to let it go?

Try listing all the cognitive biases you think contribute to you overworking (for example, underestimating how long tasks will take). Come up with a game plan for how to remove or reduce the impact of these biases. Look for heuristics that will solve more than one problem. The do-$100+ tasks-first heuristic solves virtually all problems with prioritizing for me, without needing to get more complicated than that. What would do that for you?

Get personal with yourself about what's valuable and meaningful about work to you. How can you derive most of those benefits without the costs of overworking?

Avoiding Difficult Conversations

We've talked about how an avoidant coping style is often a major factor in what holds people back. Within this general tendency, a specific habit that causes problems is avoiding difficult conversations at work. The types of conversations could be things like admitting a mistake; asking your boss for a raise, time off, or a shift in responsibilities; reaching out to people you'd like to partner with; or communicating with an employee whose work you're unhappy with.

Solutions

Grab your highlighter so you can note which of these solutions seem most useful and relevant to you.

Use the do-unto-others principle. For example, if you need to own up to a mistake or ask for time off and roles were reversed, would you rather someone did this sooner or later? Put yourself in the shoes of whomever you need to have the conversation with.

Take 50 percent responsibility for how the conversation goes, not 100 percent. Beyond taking basic steps like timing your request thoughtfully, you can be responsible for only your actions and reactions, not your conversation partner's thoughts and feelings. Thinking this way can help you not overly personalize other people's behavior.

Believe in your capacity to handle being told no. A common cognitive error is that people overestimate the potential negative consequences of making a request and it being declined. You can cope with being told no, without going into an anxiety spiral about whether you should've asked or not.

Think about what makes it easier for people to hear critical feedback. For example, using sandwich feedback (positive, then negative, then positive) and giving feedback in a way that doesn't shame or embarrass the person in front of others.

Think of having difficult conversations as a skill you can improve rather than as a personality strength you either intrinsically have or don't have. A family doctor isn't going to say, "I'm good at knees but not good at headaches." For many of us, having difficult conversations is part of our work role, just like all our other core competencies.

If appropriate, communicate when you feel unsure about how to handle a situation. For example, let's say you've been assigned to work with a different leader whom you'd prefer not to work with based on that person's reputation. You don't think the two of you are a good fit. There are alternatives available; however, you're not sure if you should give the new relationship a chance or go with your instincts and ask to be reassigned from the get-go. You could communicate all these thoughts to whoever is in charge of your leadership assignments. Framing a difficult conversation as asking someone for advice is a very useful strategy.

Learn some basic skills about negotiating. Virtually everyone needs to negotiate as part of their work role. However, many people see it as not in their wheelhouse of skills and strengths. Negotiating is an area where you can spend a very short amount of time (say, three to four hours) learning the basic principles and then have that knowledge forever. Another reason to do this is so you'll know when common negotiating tactics are being used on you. I've included some suggestions for free and quick options for learning negotiating tips at http://healthymind toolkit.com/resources.

Find out how an assertive person (someone who doesn't avoid difficult conversations) would handle the situation. For example, I'm fairly assertive, and I often find myself asking to speak to a supervisor when working with customer service. If there is a front-line rep and two levels of supervisor, I need only one yes.

I mentioned this to a friend who said, "I've never asked for a supervisor!"

Consider that in some situations, it's good to ask for what you want, and in other situations it's good to let the other party make the first offer, in case it's better than what you were going to ask for. Recognize that there is often hidden flexibility in work situations, and the "you don't know what you don't know" principle applies.

Remember that having difficult conversations can develop trust. This especially applies if you ask for (and take) your conversation partner's advice. (Recall the principle from chapter 9 that mutual influencing strengthens relationships.)

Difficult conversations have the potential to reduce other people's stress. For example, you notice that a payment due to you is late. The other party may be embarrassed about it but avoidant, anxiously waiting for you to notice. By bringing it up yourself and reaching a reasonable solution together, you relieve the other person's anxiety as well as your own.

Try not to avoid one mode of conversation entirely, such as the phone. If you have kids, consider teaching them, "If you want something, you have to call and ask. I won't do it for you." For example, calling a restaurant to place a takeout order or calling grandparents to ask if they can sleep over. Create a family culture of not avoiding the phone, and apply this principle at home and work.

The book *Difficult Conversations* is a good additional resource on this topic.[7]

Solving Your Micro-Self-Sabotaging Patterns

Back in chapter 5, we covered how small inefficiencies can add up and cost you time and frustration. Here's your prompt to look for any micro-self-sabotaging patterns you have in your work life that require only very small adjustments to solve.

For example:

If you write checklists but then don't read them, you might need to stick them on the back of your door.

If you tend to go down the rabbit hole when you're working and spend too long on one aspect of a project, you may need to give each aspect of a project a time limit.

If you have a particular cognitive bias that comes up repeatedly, you may need a reminder to refute it, such as making yourself a sign for your office wall. Someone who catastrophizes might create a reminder for themselves that problems that seem difficult initially almost always feel much easier to solve when you look at them with fresh eyes the next day. (This is a reminder I give myself when I'm feeling stressed out by something work related.)

Experiment
Try keeping a running list of any micropatterns you observe that affect your work productivity or enjoyment. Periodically, problem solve some those items that seem to have easy solutions.

Moving On

❏ What's the top single insight you want to remember from this
   chapter?

❏ Harking back to the concept that insights need to be translated into
   design changes before they affect behavior, how can you do that? For
   example:

   You set up a physical reminder of an insight you want to remember.

   You put a system in place that forces you into a hard deadline—
   for example, you hire someone to help you with the next step of a
   project with a specific start date, meaning you need to get your current step finished by then.

CHAPTER 13

. . . .

Sabotaging Patterns
Related to Money

There is a fairly short list of biases that account for most of the ways people shoot themselves in the foot when it comes to their net worth. Once you get a good handle on these patterns you'll be able to see them cropping up in your life, time and time again, in a multitude of ways. The element that the majority of these patterns share is that they cause us to overlook the big picture when it comes to our finances and our happiness.

As you read, first and foremost think about how optimizing your financial decisions could help you get the most enjoyment out of your money. Although this chapter is superficially about money, it's really about relieving unnecessary stress, achieving mental clarity, understanding the choices that will make you happiest, and minimizing the extent you need to work just to support your lifestyle.

Because life is often busy and exhausting, it's easy to distract ourselves and not feel any sense of urgency to get to money matters, especially if you feel unconfident or overwhelmed in this area. You might think, "There's always later," but later never comes. I hope reading this chapter will give you a nudge and a framework to think about your money-related decisions and that you come out of it with lots of practical takeaways. Let's look at the main cognitive biases that people commonly have when it comes to money.

Spending Less Usually Makes for an Easier, Calmer Life Immediately, Not Just in the Long Term

Don't overlook the fact that spending less usually makes for an easier, calmer life immediately, not just in the long term. Cutting spending is often framed as something painful you do begrudgingly because it's good for you. (It's interesting that exercise is often framed in the same way.) This misses the point that consuming less, and therefore reducing your spending, tends to be less stressful immediately (and often creates more free time). In other words, spending less does not need to involve giving up current happiness for future happiness. Quite the opposite.

Consider the example of devices. The more devices you have, the more items you need to keep charged, the more different types of chargers you need, the more updates you need to run, the more technological knowledge you need, and the more you'll have the urge to protect what you own against being damaged, lost, or stolen. Does this sound familiar? More broadly, the less you possess, the less you'll need to clean, store, rearrange, fix, make decisions about, and discard.

Having a home that is the perfect fit for your family, rather than oversize, is less stressful. It takes less time and energy to clean and decorate a smaller space than a larger home, and you have to work less to pay for it. If you want to make an aesthetic change to your house because your tastes change, that's also usually much cheaper and easier with a smaller house. Plus your monthly heating and cooling bills will generally be lower, and when you have to buy a new HVAC, you'll need a less powerful model.

In terms of transportation, if you have a cheap car and/or a cheap bicycle, it's not such a big deal if it gets scratched, stolen, or written off in an accident.

Inexpensive after-school activities are often less stressful for both parents and kids. Basic options like trips to the park or the neighborhood pool don't involve purchasing specialized gear or driving across town in rush hour traffic.

Although going to restaurants might be fun sometimes, anyone who has lived in a hotel (for example, for work) will tell you that eating out for every meal is extraordinarily time-consuming and expensive. On the other hand, cooking in bulk and using your freezer tends to require less money and less time.

When it comes to gifts, choosing simpler, less expensive gifts is less stressful than choosing larger gifts.

IMPORTANT!

I have no judgment if you do want a big house, a fancy car, and/or one of every type of Nintendo console ever made. The only point here is to factor in that seemingly desirable options have costs in terms of time and stress as well as money. I'm an advocate of making the more stressful choice when doing that is sufficiently personally meaningful for you. It can be difficult to write about money without it seeming like I'm advocating a particular value system for how you choose to live your life. I'm not. My goal is to help you align *your* decision making with *your* values, whatever those are.

Solutions

Use these thinking hacks to increase the sustained happiness you experience from spending your money.

Researcher Elizabeth Dunn and colleagues[1] recommend that when making purchase decisions you think about how a purchase is going to impact your life on an everyday basis, including the upsides and the downsides. For example, you're considering buying a fancy new bike. Make sure you contemplate what it's going to be like to attach a giant, hulking lock to it several times a day to prevent it being stolen. On the flip side, if a purchase is going to improve your life on a daily basis, with no downsides, that's an excellent indicator to go for it. For example, if fixing a broken item in your home will relieve you from a daily dose of frustration.

Try thinking about reducing consumption as a way to spend more time enjoying the purchases that are most pleasurable and meaningful to you. When you consume less, you can look forward to and enjoy what you buy more mindfully and guilt free.

Build delays into your spending so you can savor anticipated pleasure. Much of the enjoyment we get from spending money (and from pleasant experiences generally) comes from anticipation. For example, the positive emotions I get from planning a vacation are almost as much as those from the trip itself. An added bonus when you pause between considering and committing to a purchase is that it gives you a chance to improve your decision making. For example, you remember to check whether it's going to be the monsoon season before you've hit CONFIRM PURCHASE on a beach vacation.

Factor in the liking-versus-wanting bias.[2] What we *want* (desire) and what we *like* (enjoy having) are different, partly because two different brain systems are involved. You might strongly *want* something that becomes available to you, but once you get it you don't actually *enjoy* it enough to warrant the money or time spent acquiring and/or maintaining it. For example, when you're looking at TVs in the showroom, you may strongly *want* the biggest one, but in reality there may be only a small difference between how much you *like* watching a sixty-inch screen compared to watching a forty-nine-inch screen.

Free Isn't Really Free: Opportunity Cost

People often lose sight of money being only one type of cost. Another hugely important cost of consumption is your attention. Many free (or cheap) services are designed to be as addictive as possible. They're designed to funnel us into overconsuming, like the way the next episode starts straight after the last one on Netflix. While getting sucked into the vortex of these behaviors often feels somewhat pleasant and doesn't have a direct monetary cost, it does have an opportunity cost.

If you're not familiar with the term, *opportunity cost* refers to when you're not able to do option B because you're doing option A. If you weren't spending so much time hooked into addictive free services there's a good chance that whatever alternative you would be doing would have a more positive effect on your net worth. While you're on social media or watching TV, you're not engaging in activities that promote useful mind wandering (like taking a walk) or enjoying other hobbies or interests that might improve your problem solving, attention, relationships, physical health, or flexible thinking.

Solutions

It's easy to be self-critical and personalize overconsumption until you think about how much design goes into shaping our behavior. If the average American is spending around six hours per day consuming media via their TV or smartphone, it's not 350,000,000 people who have a personality problem.[3] Because it's not in companies' interests for us to consume less, you'll need to take the initiative to reshape your behavior yourself. There are many design changes you can make on your own behalf. For example:

You might use the Do Not Disturb (DND) setting on your phone so you're not getting notifications between certain hours. Currently, I have my phone set to DND between 10 P.M. and 10 A.M., which I find works well for me.

As an alternative or in addition, you could permanently turn off all notifications from companies but allow notifications from people (for messaging apps, for example).[4]

Try keeping only practical apps on your phone's home screen—for example, maps, note taking, and weather. Move other apps into folders on a different screen to make it less likely you'll mindlessly open them. These subtle changes make a difference, and you can use the same basic principles in many areas of your life (see www.timewellspent.io for some suggestions). For example, at Google headquarters they keep the M&M's in opaque gray jars so that they're less attention grabbing. Essentially you can do the same with your apps by dropping them into unappealing folders.

Try StayFocusd (or a similar app) if you want to become more mindful of how often you're using particular websites. Have the app block you from doing so after a certain number of minutes per day. As mentioned in chapter 5, you can always do this only temporarily to reset your default behaviors. You don't need to be all or nothing about any of the proposed solutions.

Let good habits cross-pollinate. Because we all have limited time and energy, look to make choices that will benefit you in multiple ways, including financial. Physical activity is the ideal, perhaps even prototypical, example of this. For example, walking or biking more as a mode of transportation saves money, and when you're walking you're not spending. Moreover, any physical activity, not just the intense types, makes people happier in the subsequent hours,[5] and it also enhances self-control.[6] Mentally link being active to whatever personal value you find most motivating. Note that focusing on benefits you experience immediately, rather than those you won't reap for a long time, will typically make habits more resilient. Therefore, consider focusing on any experiential benefits you personally get from physical activity, like feeling more energized or gaining insights into your life, rather than how it will benefit long-term goals. Whatever your primary reason is for being active, you'll acquire all of the other benefits from the same single behavior.

What's Marketed as a Way to Save Money Is Mostly Intended to Make You Spend More

A paradox when it comes to finances is that almost everything that's marketed as a way to help you save money is designed to increase what you spend. Some examples are sales, coupons, promo codes, credit card rewards, other reward and loyalty programs, free trials, free samples, generous returns policies, subscriptions, and free or fast shipping. Absurdly low entry pricing is another marketing tactic—you buy a deeply discounted device, but the expectation is that you'll end up buying expensive accessories or that it will hook you into a brand's ecosystem.

It's not just that these methods are used to encourage you to part with your money, they're painstakingly crafted, tested, and tweaked so that you spend the most money over time with that particular brand or company. Of course, it's possible to obtain huge value from participating in different types of incentives. However, when you're making decisions, at the very least you'll want to ensure that the brand's reason for offering the incentives and the behavioral psychology involved are at the front of your mind. Free and cheap is not free or cheap when it's designed to hook you into future spending.

Solutions

The following tips will help you become more resilient against marketing tactics that encourage overconsumption.

Unsubscribe to sales emails. You can always google for a promo or coupon code when you need one.

If you're prone to overspending (or even if you're not), you might set a personal policy of not signing up to services at free or discounted rates. If the service is worth it to you, it'll be worth it at full price. This is counterintuitive thinking, but here's why I make this argument. When membership/subscription companies give free trials or discounts for new sign ups, it triggers the *endowment effect*—our tendency to overvalue what we own or have. Let's say you receive an offer to join a warehouse club at half the usual cost. You pay $30, but the usual fee is $60. You wouldn't value joining enough to pay $60, but at $30 the reward centers of your brain light up at the sniff of a bargain. Almost regardless of how much you end up shopping at the club, when it comes time to renew at the full $60, it's more likely that you'll see doing so as worthwhile. Why? Because $60 is now the price of not *losing* your membership privileges as opposed to attaining them. Your loss aversion has kicked in (we'll talk much more about loss aversion shortly). Because of this cognitive effect, you'll want to be fairly sure that a service will be worth it to you at full price before you accept a discounted sign up offer. You'll know this from whether you'd be willing to sign up for the first time at full price or not. If you do subscribe to a free trial, at minimum, turn off auto renewal as soon as you sign up, and give yourself a month after the free or discounted trial period ends to decide if you want to sign up for a full price membership.

Pay attention to promotions that adjust upward the level of luxury you expect from your experiences. For example, hotel credit cards that offer you a free night at any level property when you sign up. These allow you to enjoy the brand's best properties. However, when you experience that luxury, chances are you're going to want it again. It's human nature. It's nice to feel, "I deserve this."

Think about where you shop. Remember that situations rather than personality often have the most impact on behavior. If you shop somewhere that mainly sells fruits and vegetables (such as inexpensive, immigrant-orientated supermarkets), what you're mainly going to buy is fruits and vegetables. Likewise, you may (or may not) find that doing your food shopping at a warehouse club results in eating more cheaply and healthfully because you buy fresh, whole foods and the ingredients used for home cooking in larger quantities. To some extent, you'll need to test your own experience and whether you're susceptible to picking up a new TV along with your two pounds of blueberries.

Accept some critiques of your spending choices. It can be easy to interpret other people's feedback on your spending as implying you don't deserve whatever it is that you want. However, there can be value to listening to other people's judgments. For example, let's say you think of dining out as part of your food budget, and someone external who overlooks your spending mentions that dining out is more about entertainment than food. If you see their point, that small cognitive shift may subtly alter your behavior and help you become more open to different choices, whether consistently or occasionally. Likewise, a curmudgeon spouse or family member who asks, "Are you getting X dollars of happiness out of that?" may help you see that you're not.

Be aware of how comparison shopping is likely to lead to you wanting fancier items with more features than you need. Comparison shopping highlights the differences between options.[7] We tend to overestimate the impact those differences will have on our happiness, hence you buy the $400 blender, instead of the $300 version, even if the $300 model has all the core features you need. When facing these decisions, do a quick back-of-the-napkin calculation to understand how much you're overpaying to avoid a small possibility you'll regret not having a feature of the expensive model. In the blender example, let's say you estimate that there's a 10 percent chance of you being seriously upset that you didn't buy the $400 version. In this case, you're logically better off risking regret. If you have the same trade-off ten times, you'd pay an extra $1,000 ($100 × 10) for the one out of ten times you deeply wished you'd made the other choice.

That's two-and-one-half times more than subsequently buying a second blender! When you put decisions into these terms it's easier to see them more rationally. Humans will pay more to avoid regret than to avoid virtually any other emotion.[8] However, you likely overestimate how bad regret would feel.

If you find your tastes are creeping up the luxury scale, try mixing in cheaper habits with more expensive ones. For example, I'll often take the bus to the airport rather than a Lyft or other rideshare. Likewise, if I'm traveling alone, I'll sometimes stay in a hostel rather than a hotel. In my twenties, these were the only ways I could afford to travel. The reason I do these behaviors now is so they don't drift out of my repertoire of normal, comfortable behaviors. I don't want to habituate to nice hotels, to the point that staying in a physically comfortable hostel becomes psychologically uncomfortable. And I want to avoid hedonic adaptation so fancy hotels still feel like a treat.

There's a relationship between being willing to tolerate physical discomfort (such as carrying items in a backpack and walking rather than taking a car) and being able to withstand emotional discomfort. Sometimes voluntarily experiencing physical discomfort, in service of your goals, will help you become more comfortable tolerating emotional discomfort. For example, starting aerobic exercise leads to lower physiological reactions to psychological stress.[9]

Buy used items often enough that doing so is in your comfort zone. For example, if you buy one used item on Craigslist (or a similar website) every three months or so, that behavior will likely stay in your repertoire. Doing this keeps the option of buying used on your radar and makes it more likely it will feel comfortable when it makes sense for a particular purchase. What do you think to buy only new that you could buy used?

Due to risk aversion, we'll overpay for the psychological comfort of minimizing any risk of problems. For example, you might be willing to pay twice as much to buy a brand name item at a traditional retailer with a generous returns policy instead of buying an off-brand version on eBay, even if there's a greater than 50 percent chance that the off-brand item will be just fine. People will dramatically overpay to avoid even the tiniest chance of unreliability, even when the purchase is small, there are no safety implications, and an absolute guarantee of reliability doesn't really matter.

Reframe what you consider normal and luxury. Early retirement blogger Pete Adeney, who runs the website Mr. Money Mustache, argues that, if you're prepared to look, you can buy a perfectly good car that will last you ten years for under $5,000 and that spending more is unnecessary.[10] Having lived in several cities previously where I relied on public transportation, having a car truly is a luxury. Whenever I think of my 2006 Honda Accord as a luxury, I smile because it's both funny and true. It's an air-conditioned chariot that takes me wherever I want to go, on demand. You don't need a luxury car if your old car is already a luxury! You might take (proven) safety features into consideration when you're making a car purchase, but beyond that, any car you buy will be a "fancy" car.[11]

Strong brands can make us susceptible to the *halo effect*, which is when an item is judged more favorably due to its association with something else. Usually the halo effect is talked about in terms of when something nonvirtuous is bundled with something virtuous. For example, people make lower estimates of the calories in a burger when the burger is served with celery sticks than when it's served without any extras, and paradoxically, people are more likely to choose indulgent menu items when there is a healthful item on the menu.[12] If we like a brand, the halo effect can make all the products made by that brand seem more desirable. If you love your expensive phone made by a certain manufacturer, it doesn't necessarily mean a tablet by the same manufacturer is the best choice. Likewise, in the investing sphere, you'd want to avoid investing in a company simply based on the fact a likable celebrity had invested.

Loss Aversion

Perhaps the biggest money bias most people have is *loss aversion*, a concept I've mentioned briefly already. The basic gist of loss aversion is that the psychological pain from losing money far outstrips the pleasurable emotions we experience from equivalent gains.[13] Losing $1 feels more painful than gaining $1 feels satisfying. Let's look at another couple of examples.

Getting charged a 10-cent surcharge when a store provides a bag generally feels worse than not receiving a 10-cent discount for bringing your own bag.

The thought of having $1,000 stolen feels far worse than the thought of not gaining $1,000 by investing or changing your habits.

A classic example that demonstrates loss aversion is the coin flip experiment: an individual is told that, if they choose to participate in the experiment and the coin comes up tails when flipped, they'll be required to pay $10. If the coin comes up heads, the participant will be given $10 instead. In general, people decline participating if the amount they'll receive for heads is less than around $20.[14] The experiment shows we are twice as sensitive to losses as we are to gains. Loss aversion results in people underinvesting and/or choosing investments that are too conservative (that don't have as much risk of periodically dropping in value but will likely provide lower returns overall).

Overcoming excessive loss aversion will put you on the fast track to rational decision making, happiness, and success. You'll have far more confidence to make the decisions that will be best for you overall. Here are some suggestions for doing that. These strategies mix trying to become less susceptible to loss aversion with assuming you *will* be vulnerable to it and using workarounds.

Solutions

Use basic math when facing loss aversion. For example, let's say you're considering booking a flight that costs $500 and has a $150 change fee if you need to alter your travel dates. You expect that the cost of the flight will rise as time passes and the chance of your needing to change your flight is around 20 percent. On average, if you booked the flight five times and paid a cancellation fee once, you'd be paying a $30 change fee per flight (20 percent of $150). Therefore if you expect the flight cost to rise more than $30, it makes logical sense to make the booking and risk the change fee. Note that whether you plan on taking five flights or not, the reasoning still holds. *Personally I have a huge aversion to change fees so I find this one very difficult!*

When it comes to investing, both undermonitoring (avoidance) and overmonitoring can be a problem. If you hold stock market investments, the more you log in and check on them, the more likely it is you'll observe a moderate (2 percent or greater) loss. Because observing a loss can cause you to deviate from your preset investing plan by pulling out your money, it makes you vulnerable to what's known as the *behavior gap*. This is when an individual investor ends up with worse returns personally than the general performance of their investment because of their attempts to time the market.[15] Obviously you wouldn't want to never monitor your investments, I'm merely pointing out that overdoing it can be a problem too. There's some evidence that extremely simple low-decision options can still be wise choices. For example, people like Warren Buffett have argued that, for nonprofessional investors, the autopilot easy option of putting your retirement savings into an index fund that tracks the stock market as a whole is also the best option.[16]

When a behavior requires you to overcome loss aversion, set that behavior to happen automatically to the greatest extent possible. For example, you plan to increase your deposits into your IRA in a few months after you've paid down some high-interest credit card debt. If possible, set up those autodeposits today, specifying that they'll start at the future date you intend. It'll be easier to commit your future self to that behavior now than it will be to commit when the time rolls around. To some extent, our current self and our future self feel like two different people, which contributes to why saving for the future is so hard in the first place![17] This way, you're using this cognitive bias to your advantage to commit your future self to a positive behavior.

If you're considering an investment, educate yourself about the frequency of losses that's normal for that investment type. Google how often the stock market loses 5, 10, 20, 30, or 50 percent. Of course, the past doesn't guarantee the future, but you can use that information as a baseline to proactively consider how you'd cope in those scenarios and what level of risk makes sense in your financial situation.

IMPORTANT!

A fascinating aspect of loss aversion is that even though, pound for pound, pain is usually more impactful than pleasure, people tolerate and bounce back from losses quicker than they expect. Therefore, when you're considering what size loss you could tolerate without panicking and withdrawing all your investment funds, recognize that you are probably underestimating your capacity. Your psychological immune system is likely better than you give yourself credit for. Use strategies to avoid a knee-jerk reaction.[18]

Loss aversion is so powerful that it can cause us to ignore other risks, particularly the risk of inaction. In terms of investing, the risk of delaying action seems smaller than it is in reality because even large percentage returns on small and moderate amounts aren't hugely exciting. If you invest $5,000 and it gains a whopping 50 percent, that's only $2,500. If investing is unfamiliar and uncomfortable for you, overcoming your fear is a lot of psychological pain to go through for $2,500. The massive gains you make from tolerating periodic losses don't come until much later.

The other side of loss aversion is that while we fear large losses, we often overlook small costs that are a slow leak but accumulate over time. For example, seemingly small differences in the fees associated with your investments can make a staggeringly large impact on your returns, all else being equal. You can get a visual representation of this by checking out the graph "Portfolio Value from Investing $100,000 over 20 Years" from the U.S. Securities and Exchange Commission (available at www.sec.gov/investor /alerts/ib_fees_expenses.pdf). In real-world terms, a fraction of a percent difference (such as investing in a fund with a 0.25 percent versus 1 percent expense ratio) may mean needing to work an extra year or more to hit your retirement goal. All this goes back to the general principle discussed in chapter 5 about how we tend to underestimate the accumulated impact of small inefficiencies over time. You can use an app (such as FeeX) to track your fees automatically and show you what you're paying in actual dollar terms.

Don't take a tendency to loss aversion personally. The cognitive biases we've been discussing are more about human nature than about you individually. There's no need to load up on shame or self-criticism. Making a good decision in the face of loss aversion is difficult to do a single time, let alone multiple times. Therefore, as previously mentioned, put "good" behaviors on autopilot to minimize the frequency with which you're asking yourself to fly in the face of your wiring.

Adopt a growth mindset[19] when it comes to understanding the ways loss aversion affects your decision making. This just means believing that you can improve your competency, rather than believing that competency is something you either have or don't have.

If you're nervous about investing, talk to people you know about how they've weathered market downturns, such as the 2008 financial crisis. Find out about what losses they experienced, how they coped, and how they bounced back.

The sunk costs trap is an offshoot of loss aversion. I've mentioned sunk costs previously in relation to time and effort. Let's look at an example that involves money: You spend $600 to fix your car only to have it break down again a few months later and need another $400 of repairs. Because you recently spent that $600, you're more likely to spend the next $400, compared to if your car needed $1,000 of repairs initially. Why? Not spending the additional $400 makes you feel like you've lost most of the value from the $600 you already spent. Even if you logically evaluate that the recurring problems are evidence that you're now throwing good money after bad, it's hard to break away psychologically from wanting to extract value from the $600 you've already spent. We also face the same sunk costs trap when we need to cancel a subscription service we've been paying for but not using. It's difficult not to think you can somehow recoup the money you've spent by using the service a lot more going forward. However, that doesn't make logical sense.

Have a Compelling Financial Goal

It's easy to overlook opportunity cost if you don't have a financial goal that's meaningful and compelling to you. This principle applies wherever you're starting from. Your current goal might be to build an emergency fund or you might have a more ambitious aim, like retiring at age forty.

Solutions

Once you have a money goal, use back-of-the-napkin calculations to quickly see how different choices you make will hasten or delay you reaching that goal. "If I'm spending $X on this, I'm not applying it to my goal, which will delay reaching my goal by Y months." Or, "If I were to do X, I could achieve my goal Y months sooner." You don't need to always choose your longer-term goal, but at least choose it some of the time.

Consider the opportunity cost of holding on to items you don't use. Let's say you have stuff sitting around your house that you don't get much value from. All told, you think you could sell these items for $1,000. Nobel Prize winner Daniel Kahneman recommends using the *overnight test* for overcoming loss aversion in this scenario.[20] Imagine that overnight someone came and replaced your items with $1,000 of cash. With that cash, would you go out and buy the exact same items again? If you wouldn't, then that's your cue to sell those items. You can use the overnight test to evaluate any type of asset you hold, even stock market investments. Ask yourself, Would I rebuy the exact same investments for the same amount I can sell them for now? Always calculate the cost of holding on to items in terms of how it impacts your main financial goal—for example, "If I made $1,000 selling my stuff on Craigslist and invested that money, I could reach my goal X months sooner."

Because loss aversion is so hard-wired, switching to more rational thinking and then following through with action is hard. Consider whether an accountability partner could be useful for getting yourself to follow through.

In economics, they talk about how money is "fungible." That amusing word might make the following concept easier to remember. *Fungible* basically means interchangeable. You can think of any money decision in terms of return on investment and opportunity cost. For example, what would be the ROI of replacing your old-style light bulbs with more energy efficient ones or improving the insulation in your home?[21] You might assess that the return would be higher than is likely from investing in the stock market, but not as high as from paying down your credit card debt. Therefore, you'd prioritize improving your home's energy efficiency *after* paying off your credit card debt but *before* investing in stocks. (You would need to do the calculation for your own circumstances. I'm speaking hypothetically here.)

If saving for retirement feels depressing to you, then the answer may be switching to a more exciting goal. Instead of retirement you could think of financial independence. This is the point where you can perpetually draw enough income from your investments to completely support your spending, and you no longer need to work to earn income. You may still choose to work for other reasons. There's some modeling that suggests that to be financially independent you need to have twenty-five to twenty-eight times your annual spending needs in investments (for a more in-depth explanation see "The 4% Rule").[22] You'd need $1 million if you spend $35–40K a year, but $2 million if you spend $70–80K a year. According to the theory, once your investments reach that level, you'd be a completely free person from a financial standpoint. There's a high likelihood that you could withdraw what you need to live on every year for decades without running out of money.

Another way to think about the math of financial independence is that if you invest 50 percent of your income you can potentially go from zero to being fully financially independent in sixteen years. If you save only 5 percent of your income, it would take more than fifty years.[23] I'm not an investment adviser, so you should do your research and reach your own conclusions, but these are interesting, alternative ways to think about retirement savings. Certain choices, like working until you're in your mid-sixties or older, seem normal because that's what most other people do, but there are also other options. This is an example of when thinking bigger may be necessary for motivation. Bigger goals are not necessarily harder than smaller goals. Saving 50 percent of your income might actually be easier than saving lower amounts because the goal is more inspiring, and it forces a dramatic paradigm shift in how you spend.

Saving money and gaining more free time often align. However, if you need to make a trade-off, there's some research evidence that valuing time over money makes us happier.[24]

Troubleshoot Unwillingness to Tolerate Psychological Discomfort

We've already covered some examples of how being unwilling to tolerate psychological discomfort can lead to poor money choices, such as giving in to fear and never investing. What other ways does this manifest for you? Let's say you feel envy in relation to a friend who just went on vacation and traveled in business class. For your next trip, you book a business seat for yourself, even though you can't really afford it. Or you overspend when you're feeling bored, tired, or lonely. Check out the suggestions in chapter 4 for coping with uncomfortable emotions in adaptive ways.

If you tend toward being anxious, a particular quirk to be aware of is that anxious people will prefer certainty to uncertainty, even if there is no risk of loss per se *and* there is a good chance that the more uncertain option will be more lucrative.[25] For example, take a scenario in which you can choose to trade your car in to a dealer for a low but certain price. If you sold your car yourself, you'd have less certainty about how long it would take to sell or how much it would sell for. However, you assess that you're likely to come out ahead, and if not, you could always go back to sell it to the dealer. That option isn't going away. If you're willing to emotionally tolerate an uncertain situation, you can pursue the better-paying option. Understand your personal patterns and come up with a plan for preventing money mistakes that are due to unwillingness to tolerate temporary anxiety and uncertainty.

Penny Wise, but Pound Foolish

I'm going to close out the chapter with some tips for the underspender. Money tips tend to be aimed at the overspender, yet being *penny wise, but pound foolish* can be just as detrimental to your overall financial picture and/or your life satisfaction. Here are some of the self-defeating patterns associated with this tendency. Place a checkmark next to anything you relate to. The person:

Doesn't take into account nonmonetary costs in decisions. For example, they book a flight with two connections that results in arriving at their destination exhausted, when they could've arrived refreshed for $50 more.

Drives extra time to make small savings. They drive across town to save $5.

Skimps on purchasing tools, when the return clearly exceeds the investment.

Delays buying something they need until it's on sale for the desired price, even when this creates unnecessary stress and inconvenience.

Does tasks themselves that would be done more competently by an expert at a very cheap price compared to the personal time taken. They're rigidly a DIY type and might not consider the opportunity cost of DIY: that there may be more financially or psychologically lucrative options for how else they could be spending their time.

Has relationship arguments about small amounts of money.

Is controlling about money. They prevent their partner from spending money on reasonable home upgrades when there is no reason to be so controlling.

Avoids doing maintenance if it incurs a cost, resulting in either living in poorly maintained surroundings and/or incurring a larger cost that could've been avoided with appropriate maintenance.

Is very loss averse and keeps large amounts of money as cash.

Spends a lot of time managing small amounts of money when large amounts aren't optimized. They go out of their way to buy a discount brand over a nicer, more expensive brand, but they haven't asked for a pay increase in years.

Solutions

Try making a short list of why is money important to you. For example, you want to be able to pay for healthcare without thinking about it, have fast internet, eat food you enjoy, and travel to see friends and family.

For the penny wise, pound foolish person, it's not so much stressing about small amounts that is the problem, it's that the big stuff is not getting attended to. Therefore, much of the advice elsewhere in the chapter that is aimed at helping people see the big picture will apply.

In particular, make sure you're calculating the opportunity cost of your choices. For example, opting for prepared foods might help you do an extra hour of needed work on a particular day. Flexibly shift priorities rather than always sticking to the same choices.

Use solutions that get 80 percent of the benefit. For instance, I use the Walmart Savings Catcher app that automatically price matches grocery items (aside from fresh produce) to other stores. This achieves much of the benefit of shopping around or couponing, with an order of magnitude less time and effort.

Be willing to get it wrong. How often are you willing to regret a purchase? What's the value of faster decision making?

If you want to spend more freely on luxuries you enjoy, figure out what gets your brain's reward centers activated. For example, if I've bought a gift card at a discount (to use myself), I feel good about the discount and end up spending more overall at that store than if I hadn't bought the gift card. If the advice for the overspender is to scale back participating in promotions, for the underspender it's the reverse. It's easier to spend "funny money" like gift cards, miles, or points, than it is to spend real money.

Don't think your time has value only if you're spending it on paid work. One of the roadblocks to people assigning a monetary value to their time is that most people aren't going to spend an extra hour at work if they, say, hire someone to clean their house. Remember that we need time for pleasure and relaxation to be able to see all our options, make connections between different types of information, and clear our minds enough to make good decisions (not to mention to enjoy life).

Moving On

❏ Of all the material in this chapter, what seems most immediately useful to you?

❏ What insights did you find interesting but, as yet, you haven't made a plan for how you'll apply that insight. Make one plan now.

Epilogue

Congratulations on making it to the end of the book! This is your nudge to go back to the goal you set while reading chapter 1 and evaluate how closely you've achieved that.

If you didn't set a goal, you have another opportunity to do that now. I'll make a single suggestion so you don't get overwhelmed by too much choice: Pick five insights you want to apply in your life. To choose, look over any highlights or notes you've made. Don't get too hung up on what you select. Any five insights that appeal are fine.

Once you've done that, here are two other recommendations for how to continue breaking free of your self-sabotaging patterns as well as how to prevent falling back into old habits.

Going Forward: Do a Weekly Check-In

I recommend that you do a weekly self-check-in during which you look back over the prior week. If you've done any self-sabotage, identify how you could've acted differently. What strategies from the book (or of your own) could you have applied?

During your check-in, also look forward to the upcoming week and what opportunities you have to translate the insights and strategies you've read about into action. Prioritize behaviors where acting once will result in ongoing payoffs, without your needing to keep up repeated effort. Make sure you consider the various domains of your life: personal self-regulation (pleasure, health, etc.), organization, relationships, money, and work.

Consider Rereading This Book in Six or Twelve Months

We've covered a lot of ground together. If you reread the material after a few months of applying your favorite insights, you'll come back to it with a different perspective. You'll likely pick up new insights on rereading, and connect the material with your life and behavior in fresh ways.

Wrapping Up

Thanks for taking this journey with me. I encourage you to take the road map I've provided and make it your own. Get creative! I hope that what you've learned here helps you flourish in pursuing whatever is most meaningful and important to you.

NOTES

CHAPTER 1

1   Butler et al., "Empirical Status"; Hofmann and Smits, "Cognitive-Behavioral Therapy"; Newby et al., "Systematic Review"; and Tolin, "Cognitive-Behavioral Therapy."

2   Gilbert, "Introducing Compassion-Focused Therapy"; Gilbert and Procter, "Compassionate Mind Training"; and Rector et al., "Self-Criticism and Dependency."

3   Kashdan, *Curious?*

CHAPTER 2

1   Aldao and Nolen-Hoeksema, "Specificity of Cognitive Emotion."

2   Lyubomirsky, "Hedonic Adaptation."

3   Abramowitz and Foa, "Worries and Obsessions"; Salkovskis, "Obsessional-Compulsive Problems"; and Startup and Davey, "Inflated Responsibility."

4   Oettingen et al., "Pleasure Now."

5   Boyes, *Anxiety Toolkit.*

6   Goncalo et al., "Two Narcissists."

7   Schwartz, *Magic of Thinking Big.*

8   Baer, "What Good Is Hope?"; and Baer, "Why Psychologists Say."

9   Wesnousky et al., "Holding a Silver Lining Theory."

CHAPTER 3

1   Dugas et al., "Intolerance of Uncertainty."

2   Newman and Llera, "Novel Theory."

3   Read and Loewenstein, "Diversification Bias."

4   Duckworth et al., "Self-Regulation Strategies"; Stadler et al., "Intervention Effects"; and Stadler et al., "Physical Activity in Women."

5   Norem and Chang, "Positive Psychology."

6   Rubin, *Better Than Before.*

CHAPTER 4

1   Wikipedia, "Premack's Principle."

2   Kashdan and McKnight, "Commitment to a Purpose in Life."

3   Rios et al., "Attitude Certainty."

4   Forgas and East, "On Being Happy."

5   Kappes et al., "Sad Mood."

6   Barrett, *How Emotions Are Made.*

7   Kashdan et al., "Unpacking Emotion Differentiation."

8   Brackett et al., "Enhancing Academic Performance"; and Hagelskamp et al., "Improving Classroom Quality."

9 Chen and Hong, "Intolerance of Uncertainty"; Einstein, "Extension of the Transdiagnostic Model"; and Gentes and Ruscio, "Meta-Analysis of the Relation of Intolerance."

10 Kashdan and Rottenberg, "Psychological Flexibility."

11 Goulston and Goldberg, *Get Out of Your Own Way.*

CHAPTER 5

1 Baumeister and Vohs, "Strength Model of Self-Regulation."

2 Rubin, "Quiz."

3 Guillebeau, "Tips for Stress Free Travel."

4 Allen and Fallows, *Getting Things Done.*

CHAPTER 6

1 Aldao et al., "Emotion-Regulation Strategies."

2 Kashdan and Biswas-Diener, *Upside of Your Dark Side.*

3 Fredrickson, "Gratitude"; and Fredrickson, "What Good Are Positive Emotions?"

4 Guillebeau, "Brief Guide to World Domination."

5 Hayes, *Get Out of Your Mind.*

6 Kappes and Oettingen, "Positive Fantasies."

7 Prochaska and DiClemente, "Transtheoretical Therapy"; and Prochaska et al., "Stages of Change."

CHAPTER 7

1 Marlatt and Gordon, *Relapse Prevention.*

2   Rubin, *Better Than Before.*

3   McKay et al., *Mind and Emotions.*

4   Rubin, "Which of These?"

5   Harris and Hayes, *Happiness Trap.*

6   Zabelina and Robinson, "Don't Be So Hard."

7   Beck and Beck, *Cognitive Behavior Therapy.*

8   Kuziemko, "Is Having Babies Contagious?"

CHAPTER 8

1   Nickerson, "Confirmation Bias."

2   Wikipedia, "Big Five Personality Traits."

3   Hunter and Cushenbery, "Is Being a Jerk Necessary?"

4   Alexandrov, Lilly, and Babakus, "Effects of Social- and Self-Motives."

5   Bernhard and Boorstein, *How to Be Sick.*

6   Pronin, Lin, and Ross, "Bias Blind Spot."

7   Brown, "Better Than Average Effect."

8   Weinstein, "Unrealistic Optimism."

CHAPTER 9

1   Lyubomirsky, *The How of Happiness.*

2   Gottman and Silver, *Seven Principles.*

3   Johnson, *Emotionally Focused Couple Therapy.*

4   Jose et al., "Does Savoring Increase Happiness?"

5   Rubin, *Happiness Project.*

6   Gable et al., "Will You Be There?"

7   Kashdan et al., "Failure to Capitalize."

8   Murray et al., "Self-Fulfilling Nature."

9   Aron et al., "Experimental Generation of Interpersonal Closeness."

10   Wikipedia, "False Consensus Effect."

11   Winch, *Emotional First Aid.*

12   Christensen et al., *Reconcilable Differences.*

CHAPTER 10

1   Konrath et al., "Changes in Adult Attachment Styles"; and Mickelson et al., "Adult Attachment."

2   Fraley, "Attachment Stability"; and Waters et al., "Stability of Attachment Security."

3   Kirkpatrick and Hazan, "Attachment Styles and Close Relationships"; and Waters et al., "Stability of Attachment Security."

4   Tatkin and Hendrix, *Wired for Love.*

5   Tatkin and Hendrix, *Wired for Love.*

6   Levine and Heller, *Attached.*

7   Tatkin and Hendrix, *Wired for Love.*

8   Griffin and Bartholomew, "Models of the Self and Other."

9   MacDonald and Borsook, "Attachment Avoidance."

10   Carvallo and Gabriel, "No Man Is an Island."

11   Gottman and Silver, *Seven Principles*.

12   Winch, *Emotional First Aid*.

13   Girme et al., "'All or Nothing.'"

14   Overall et al., "Buffering Attachment-Related Avoidance."

CHAPTER 11

1   Welch and Houser, "Extending the Four-Category Model"; and You and Malley-Morrison, "Young Adult Attachment Styles."

2   Bippus and Rollin, "Attachment Style Differences."

3   Welch and Houser, "Extending the Four-Category Model."

4   Saferstein et al., "Attachment as a Predictor."

5   Chango et al., "Attachment Organization and Patterns."

6   Shomaker and Furman, "Parent-Adolescent Relationship Qualities."

7   Hardy and Barkham, "Relationship between Interpersonal Attachment Styles."

8   Berson et al., "Attachment Style and Individual Differences."

9   Little et al., "Integrating Attachment Style."

10   Pines, "Adult Attachment Styles."

11   Krausz et al., "Effects of Attachment Style."

12   Davidovitz et al., "Leaders as Attachment Figures."

13   Johnston, "Delegation and Organizational Structure."

14   Erozkan, "Relationship between Attachment Styles."

15   Davidovitz et al., "Leaders as Attachment Figures."

16   Boatwright et al., "Influence of Adult Attachment Styles."

17   Towler and Stuhlmacher, "Attachment Styles."

18   Ein-Dor and Tal, "Scared Saviors."

19   Gillath et al., "Attachment-Style Differences."

CHAPTER 12

1   Boyes, *Anxiety Toolkit.*

2   Clance and Imes, "Imposter Phenomenon."

3   Egan et al., "Perfectionism as a Transdiagnostic Process."

4   Nickerson, "How We Know."

5   Kashdan and Biswas-Diener, *Upside of Your Dark Side.*

6   Ferriss, *4-Hour Workweek.*

7   Stone et al., *Difficult Conversations.*

CHAPTER 13

1   Dunn et al., "If Money Doesn't Make You Happy."

2   Berridge et al., "Dissecting Components of Reward."

3   Howard, "Americans at More."

4   "Take Control."

5   Lathia et al., "Happier People."

6   Oaten and Cheng, "Longitudinal Gains."

7   Dunn and Norton, *Happy Money.*

8   Lau et al., "Quantifying the Value."

9   Von Haaren et al., "20-Week Aerobic Exercise."

10   Ferriss, "Mr. Money Mustache."

11   Lehrer, "'New World Order.'"

12   Chernev, "Dieter's Paradox"; and Wilcox et al., "Vicarious Goal Fulfillment."

13   Kahneman and Tversky, "Choices, Values, and Frames."

14   Richards, "Overcoming an Aversion to Loss."

15   Egan, "High-Frequency Monitoring."

16   Buffett, "Berkshire Hathaway Inc. Shareholder Letter 2013"; and Buffett, "Berkshire Hathaway Inc. Shareholder Letter 2016."

17   McGonigal, *Willpower Instinct.*

18   Dunn et al., "If Money Doesn't Make You Happy."

19   Dweck, *Mindset.*

20   Richards, "Overcoming an Aversion to Loss."

21   Adeney, "Beating the Stock Market."

22   Adeney, "4% Rule."

23   Adeney, "4% Rule."

24   Hershfield et al., "People Who Choose Time."

25   Charpentier et al., "Enhanced Risk Aversion."

REFERENCES

Abramowitz, Jonathan S., and Edna B. Foa. "Worries and Obsessions in Individuals with Obsessive-Compulsive Disorder with and without Comorbid Generalized Anxiety Disorder." *Behaviour Research and Therapy* 36(7–8) (Aug. 1, 1998): 695–700.

Adeney, Pete. "Beating the Stock Market—With DIY Insulation." *Mr. Money Mustache* (blog). May 1, 2014. http://www.mrmoneymustache.com /2014/05/01/beating-the-stock-market-with-diy-insulation.

———. "The 4% Rule: The Easy Answer to 'How Much Do I Need for Retirement?'" *Mr. Money Mustache* (blog). May 29, 2012. http://www.mrmoney mustache.com/2012/05/29/how-much-do-i-need-for-retirement.

Aldao, Amelia, and Susan Nolen-Hoeksema. "Specificity of Cognitive Emotion Regulation Strategies: A Transdiagnostic Examination." *Behaviour Research and Therapy* 48(10) (Oct. 2010): 974–83.

Aldao, Amelia, Susan Nolen-Hoeksema, and Susanne Schweizer. "Emotion-Regulation Strategies across Psychopathology: A Meta-Analytic Review." *Clinical Psychology Review* 30(2) (Mar. 2010): 217–37.

Alexandrov, Aliosha, Bryan Lilly, and Emin Babakus. "The Effects of Social- and Self-Motives on the Intentions to Share Positive and Negative Word of Mouth." *Journal of the Academy of Marketing Science* 41(5) (Sept. 1, 2013): 531–46.

Allen, David, and James Fallows. *Getting Things Done: The Art of Stress-Free Productivity*. Rev. ed. New York: Penguin Books, 2015.

Aron, Arthur, Edward Melinat, Elaine N. Aron, Robert Darrin Vallone, and Renee J. Bator. "The Experimental Generation of Interpersonal Closeness: A Procedure and Some Preliminary Findings." *Personality and Social Psychology Bulletin* 23(4) (Apr. 1, 1997): 363–77.

Baer, Drake. "What Good Is Hope?" Science of Us (blog). *New York Magazine*, Dec. 27, 2016. http://nymag.com/scienceofus/2016/12/is-hope-good-for-you.html.

———. "Why Psychologists Say Anxiety Is the 'Shadow' of Intelligence." Science of Us (blog). *New York Magazine*, September 15, 2016. http://nymag.com/scienceofus/2016/09/psychologists-say-anxiety-is-the-shadow-of-intelligence.html.

Barrett, Lisa Feldman. *How Emotions Are Made: The Secret Life of the Brain.* New York: Houghton Mifflin Harcourt, 2017.

Baumeister, Roy, and Kathleen D. Vohs. "Strength Model of Self-Regulation as Limited Resource." In *Advances in Experimental Social Psychology*, vol. 54, edited by James M. Olson and Mark P. Zanna, 67–127. New York: Elsevier, 2016.

Beck, Judith S., and Aaron T. Beck. *Cognitive Behavior Therapy: Basics and Beyond.* 2nd ed. New York: Guilford Press, 2011.

Bernhard, Toni, and Sylvia Boorstein. *How to Be Sick: A Buddhist-Inspired Guide for the Chronically Ill and Their Caregivers.* Boston: Wisdom, 2010.

Berridge, Kent C., Terry E. Robinson, and J. Wayne Aldridge. "Dissecting Components of Reward: 'Liking,' 'Wanting,' and Learning." *Current Opinion in Pharmacology* 9(1) (Feb. 2009): 65–73.

Berson, Yair, Orrie Dan, and Francis J. Yammarino. "Attachment Style and Individual Differences in Leadership Perceptions and Emergence." *Journal of Social Psychology* 146(2) (Apr. 1, 2006): 165–82.

Bippus, Amy M., and Emma Rollin. "Attachment Style Differences in Relational Maintenance and Conflict Behaviors: Friends' Perceptions." *Communication Reports* 16(2) (Jun. 1, 2003): 113–23.

Boatwright, Karyn J., Frederick G. Lopez, Eric M. Sauer, Abbie VanDerWege, and Daniel M. Huber. "The Influence of Adult Attachment Styles on Workers' Preferences for Relational Leadership Behaviors." *Psychologist-Manager Journal* 13(1) (Feb. 5, 2010): 1–14.

Boyes, Alice. *The Anxiety Toolkit: Strategies for Fine-Tuning Your Mind and Moving Past Your Stuck Points.* New York: TarcherPerigee, 2015.

Brackett, Marc A., Susan E. Rivers, Maria R. Reyes, and Peter Salovey. "Enhancing Academic Performance and Social and Emotional Competence with the RULER Feeling Words Curriculum." *Learning and Individual Differences* 22(2) (Apr. 2012): 218–24.

Brown, Jonathon D. "Understanding the Better Than Average Effect: Motives (Still) Matter." *Personality and Social Psychology Bulletin* 38(2) (Feb. 1, 2012): 209–19.

Buffett, Warren. Shareholder letter, Berkshire Hathaway Inc. February 28, 2014. http://www.berkshirehathaway.com/letters/2013ltr.pdf.

———. Shareholder letter, Berkshire Hathaway Inc. February 25, 2017. http://www.berkshirehathaway.com/letters/2016ltr.pdf.

Butler, Andrew C., Jason E. Chapman, Evan M. Forman, and Aaron T. Beck. "The Empirical Status of Cognitive-Behavioral Therapy: A Review of Meta-Analyses." *Clinical Psychology Review* 26(1) (Jan. 2006): 17–31.

Carvallo, Mauricio, and Shira Gabriel. "No Man Is an Island: The Need to Belong and Dismissing Avoidant Attachment Style." *Personality & Social Psychology Bulletin* 32(5) (May 2006): 697–709.

Centre for Clinical Interventions. Consumer Resources. Accessed March 11, 2017. http://www.cci.health.wa.gov.au/resources/consumers.cfm.

Chango, Joanna M., Kathleen Boykin McElhaney, and Joseph P. Allen. "Attachment Organization and Patterns of Conflict Resolution in Friendships Predicting Adolescents' Depressive Symptoms Over Time." *Attachment & Human Development* 11(4) (Jul. 1, 2009): 331–46.

Charpentier, Caroline J., Jessica Aylward, Jonathan P. Roiser, and Oliver J. Robinson. "Enhanced Risk Aversion, but Not Loss Aversion, in Unmedicated Pathological Anxiety." *Biological Psychiatry* 81(12) (Jun. 15, 2017): 1014–1022.

Chen, Charlene Y., and Ryan Y. Hong. "Intolerance of Uncertainty Moderates the Relation between Negative Life Events and Anxiety." *Personality and Individual Differences* 49(1) (Jul. 2010): 49–53.

Chernev, Alexander. "The Dieter's Paradox." *Journal of Consumer Psychology* 21, no. 2 (Apr. 2011): 178–83.

Christensen, Andrew, Brian D. Doss, and Neil S. Jacobson. *Reconcilable Differences: Rebuild Your Relationship by Rediscovering the Partner You Love—without Losing Yourself.* 2nd. ed. New York: Guilford Press, 2014.

Clance, Pauline R., and Suzanne A. Imes. "The Imposter Phenomenon in High Achieving Women: Dynamics and Therapeutic Intervention." *Psychotherapy: Theory, Research & Practice* 15(3) (Fall 1978): 241–47.

Davidovitz, Rivka, Mario Mikulincer, Phillip R. Shaver, Ronit Izsak, and Micha Popper. "Leaders as Attachment Figures: Leaders' Attachment Orientations Predict Leadership-Related Mental Representations and Followers' Performance and Mental Health." *Journal of Personality and Social Psychology* 93(4) (Oct. 2007): 632–50.

Duckworth, Angela Lee, Heidi Grant, Benjamin Loew, Gabriele Oettingen, and Peter M. Gollwitzer. "Self-Regulation Strategies Improve

Self-Discipline in Adolescents: Benefits of Mental Contrasting and Implementation Intentions." *Educational Psychology* 31(1) (Jan. 1, 2011): 17–26.

Dugas, Michel J., Mark H. Freeston, and Robert Ladouceur. "Intolerance of Uncertainty and Problem Orientation in Worry." *Cognitive Therapy and Research* 21(6) (Dec. 1, 1997): 593–606.

Dunn, Elizabeth W., Daniel T. Gilbert, and Timothy D. Wilson. "If Money Doesn't Make You Happy, Then You Probably Aren't Spending It Right." *Journal of Consumer Psychology* 21(2) (Apr. 2011): 115–25.

Dunn, Elizabeth, and Michael Norton. *Happy Money: The Science of Happier Spending.* Rpnt. ed. New York: Simon & Schuster, 2013.

Dweck, Carol S. *Mindset: The New Psychology of Success.* Updated ed. New York: Random House, 2006.

Egan, Dan. "High-Frequency Monitoring: A Short-Sighted Behavior." Betterment (website). September 16, 2014. http://www.betterment.com/resources/investment-strategy/behavioral-finance-investing-strategy/high-frequency-monitoring.

Egan, Sarah J., Tracey D. Wade, and Roz Shafran. "Perfectionism as a Transdiagnostic Process: A Clinical Review." *Clinical Psychology Review* 31(2) (March 2011): 203–12.

Ein-Dor, Tsachi, and Orgad Tal. "Scared Saviors: Evidence That People High in Attachment Anxiety Are More Effective in Alerting Others to Threat." *European Journal of Social Psychology* 42(6) (Oct. 1, 2012): 667–71.

Einstein, Danielle A. "Extension of the Transdiagnostic Model to Focus on Intolerance of Uncertainty: A Review of the Literature and Implications for Treatment." *Clinical Psychology: Science and Practice* 21(3) (Sept. 1, 2014): 280–300.

Erozkan, Atilgan. "The Relationship between Attachment Styles and Social Anxiety: An Investigation with Turkish University Students." *Social Behavior and Personality* 37(6) (Jul. 1, 2009): 835–44.

Ferriss, Timothy. *The 4-Hour Workweek: Escape 9–5, Live Anywhere, and Join the New Rich.* New York: Harmony, 2009.

Ferriss, Timothy. "Mr. Money Mustache—Living Beautifully on $25–27K Per Year." *The Tim Ferriss Show* (podcast). Episode 221. February 13, 2017. http://tim.blog/2017/02/13/mr-money-mustache.

Forgas, Joseph P., and Rebekah East. "On Being Happy and Gullible: Mood Effects on Skepticism and the Detection of Deception." *Journal of Experimental Social Psychology* 44(5) (Sept. 2008): 1362–67.

Fraley, Chris R. "Attachment Stability from Infancy to Adulthood: Meta-Analysis and Dynamic Modeling of Developmental Mechanisms." *Personality and Social Psychology Review* 6(2) (May 1, 2002): 123–51.

Fredrickson, Barbara L. "Gratitude, Like Other Positive Emotions, Broadens and Builds." In *The Psychology of Gratitude*, edited by R. A. Emmons and M. E. McCullough, 145–66. Series in Affective Science. New York: Oxford University Press, 2004.

———. "What Good Are Positive Emotions?" *Review of General Psychology* 2(3) (1998): 300–19.

Gable, Shelly L., Gian C. Gonzaga, and Amy Strachman. "Will You Be There for Me When Things Go Right? Supportive Responses to Positive Event Disclosures." *Journal of Personality and Social Psychology* 91(5) (Nov. 2006): 904–17.

Gander, Manuela, and Anna Buchheim. "Attachment Classification, Psychophysiology and Frontal EEG Asymmetry across the Lifespan: A Review." *Frontiers in Human Neuroscience* 9 (Feb. 19, 2015): 79.

Gentes, Emily L., and Ayelet Meron Ruscio. "A Meta-Analysis of the Relation of Intolerance of Uncertainty to Symptoms of Generalized Anxiety Disorder, Major Depressive Disorder, and Obsessive-Compulsive Disorder." *Clinical Psychology Review* 31(6) (Aug. 2011): 923–33.

Gilbert, Paul. "Introducing Compassion-Focused Therapy." *Advances in Psychiatric Treatment* 15(3) (May 1, 2009): 199–208.

Gilbert, Paul, and Sue Procter. "Compassionate Mind Training for People with High Shame and Self-Criticism: Overview and Pilot Study of a Group Therapy Approach." *Clinical Psychology & Psychotherapy* 13(6) (Nov. 1, 2006): 353–79.

Gillath, Omri, Silvia A. Bunge, Phillip R. Shaver, Carter Wendelken, and Mario Mikulincer. "Attachment-Style Differences in the Ability to Suppress Negative Thoughts: Exploring the Neural Correlates." *Neuroimage* 28(4) (Dec. 2005): 835–47.

Girme, Yuthika U., Nickola C. Overall, Jeffry A. Simpson, and Garth J. O. Fletcher. "'All or Nothing': Attachment Avoidance and the Curvilinear Effects of Partner Support." *Journal of Personality and Social Psychology* 108(3) (2015): 450–75.

Goncalo, Jack A., Francis J. Flynn, and Sharon H. Kim. "Are Two Narcissists Better Than One? The Link between Narcissism, Perceived Creativity, and Creative Performance." *Personality and Social Psychology Bulletin* 36(11) (Nov. 1, 2010): 1484–95.

Gottman, John, and Nan Silver. *The Seven Principles for Making Marriage Work: A Practical Guide from the Country's Foremost Relationship Expert.* Rev. ed. New York: Harmony, 2015.

Goulston, Mark, and Philip Goldberg. *Get Out of Your Own Way: Overcoming Self-Defeating Behavior.* Reissue ed. New York: TarcherPerigee, 1996.

Griffin, Dale W., and Kim Bartholomew. "Models of the Self and Other: Fundamental Dimensions Underlying Measures of Adult Attachment." *Journal of Personality and Social Psychology* 67(3) (Sept. 1994): 430–45.

Guillebeau, Chris. "A Brief Guide to World Domination (and Other Important Goals): How to Live a Remarkable Life in a Conventional World." 2008. *Chris Buillebeau* (blog). https://chrisguillebeau.com/files/2008/06/worlddomination.pdf.

Guillebeau, Chris. "Tips for Stress Free Travel." *Chris Buillebeau* (blog). https://chrisguillebeau.com/tips-for-stress-free-travel.

Hagelskamp, Carolin, Marc A. Brackett, Susan E. Rivers, and Peter Salovey. "Improving Classroom Quality with the RULER Approach to Social and Emotional Learning: Proximal and Distal Outcomes." *American Journal of Community Psychology* 51(3–4) (Jun. 2013): 530–43.

Hardy, Gillian E., and Michael Barkham. "The Relationship between Interpersonal Attachment Styles and Work Difficulties." *Human Relations* 47(3) (Mar. 1, 1994): 263–81.

Harris, Russ, and Steven Hayes. *The Happiness Trap: How to Stop Struggling and Start Living: A Guide to ACT.* Boston: Trumpeter, 2008.

Hayes, Steven C. *Get Out of Your Mind and into Your Life: The New Acceptance and Commitment Therapy.* Oakland, CA: New Harbinger, 2005.

Hershfield, Hal E., Cassie Mogilner, and Uri Barnea. "People Who Choose Time over Money Are Happier." *Social Psychological and Personality Science* 7(7) (Sept. 1, 2016): 697–706.

Hofmann, Stefan G., and Jasper A. J. Smits. "Cognitive-Behavioral Therapy for Adult Anxiety Disorders: A Meta-Analysis of Randomized Placebo-Controlled Trials." *Journal of Clinical Psychiatry* 69(4) (Apr. 2008): 621–32.

Howard, Jacqueline. "Americans at More Than 10 Hours a Day on Screens." CNN (website). June 29, 2016. http://www.cnn.com/2016/06/30/health/americans-screen-time-nielsen/index.html.

Hunter, Samuel T., and Lily Cushenbery. "Is Being a Jerk Necessary for Originality? Examining the Role of Disagreeableness in the Sharing and Utilization of Original Ideas." *Journal of Business and Psychology* 30(4) (Dec. 1, 2015): 621–39.

Johnson, Susan M. *The Practice of Emotionally Focused Couple Therapy: Creating Connection*. 2d ed. New York: Routledge, 2004.

Johnston, Michelle A. "Delegation and Organizational Structure in Small Businesses: Influences of Manager's Attachment Patterns." *Group & Organization Management* 25(1) (Mar. 1, 2000): 4–21.

Jose, Paul E., Bee T. Lim, and Fred B. Bryant. "Does Savoring Increase Happiness? A Daily Diary Study." *Journal of Positive Psychology* 7, no. 3 (May 1, 2012): 176–87.

Kahneman, Daniel, and Amos Tversky. "Choices, Values, and Frames." *American Psychologist* 39(4) (Apr. 1984): 341–50.

Kappes, Heather Barry, and Gabriele Oettingen. "Positive Fantasies about Idealized Futures Sap Energy." *Journal of Experimental Social Psychology* 47(4) (Jul. 2011): 719–29.

Kappes, Heather Barry, Gabriele Oettingen, Doris Mayer, and Sam Maglio. "Sad Mood Promotes Self-Initiated Mental Contrasting of Future and Reality." *Emotion* 11(5) (Oct. 2011): 1206–22.

Kashdan, Todd B. *Curious?: Discover the Missing Ingredient to a Fulfilling Life*. Rpnt. ed. New York: HarperCollins ebooks, 2009.

Kashdan, Todd B., Leah Adams, Juliana Read, and Larry Hawk Jr. "Can a One-Hour Session of Exposure Treatment Modulate Startle Response and Reduce Spider Fears?" *Psychiatry Research* 196(1) (Mar. 30, 2012): 79–82.

Kashdan, Todd B., Lisa Feldman Barrett, and Patrick E. McKnight. "Unpacking Emotion Differentiation: Transforming Unpleasant Experience by Perceiving Distinctions in Negativity." *Current Directions in Psychological Science* 24(1) (Feb. 1, 2015): 10–16.

Kashdan, Todd B., and Robert Biswas-Diener. *The Upside of Your Dark Side: Why Being Your Whole Self—Not Just Your "Good" Self—Drives Success and Fulfillment.* Rpnt. ed. New York: Plume, 2015.

Kashdan, Todd B., Patty Ferssizidis, Antonina S. Farmer, Leah M. Adams, and Patrick E. McKnight. "Failure to Capitalize on Sharing Good News with Romantic Partners: Exploring Positivity Deficits of Socially Anxious People with Self-Reports, Partner-Reports, and Behavioral Observations." *Behaviour Research and Therapy* 51(10) (Oct. 2013): 656–68.

Kashdan, Todd B., and Patrick E. McKnight. "Commitment to a Purpose in Life: An Antidote to the Suffering by Individuals with Social Anxiety Disorder." *Emotion* 13(6) (2013): 1150–59.

Kashdan, Todd B., and Jonathan Rottenberg. "Psychological Flexibility as a Fundamental Aspect of Health." *Clinical Psychology Review, Positive Clinical Psychology* 30(7) (Nov. 2010): 865–78.

Kirkpatrick, Lee A., and Cindy Hazan. "Attachment Styles and Close Relationships: A Four-Year Prospective Study." *Personal Relationships* 1(2) (Jun. 1, 1994): 123–42.

Konrath, Sara H., William J. Chopik, Courtney K. Hsing, and Ed O'Brien. "Changes in Adult Attachment Styles in American College Students over Time: A Meta-Analysis." *Personality and Social Psychology Review* 18(4) (Nov. 1, 2014): 326–48.

Krausz, Moshe, Aharon Bizman, and Doron Braslavsky. "Effects of Attachment Style on Preferences for and Satisfaction with Different Employment Contracts: An Exploratory Study." *Journal of Business and Psychology* 16(2) (Dec. 1, 2001): 299–316.

Kuziemko, Ilyana. "Is Having Babies Contagious? Estimating Fertility Peer Effects between Siblings." Unpublished manuscript. Harvard University, 2006. https://pdfs.semanticscholar.org/d04c/26aaf082297f6df0e6d090 b78260382345d3.pdf.

Lathia, Neal, Gillian M. Sandstrom, Cecilia Mascolo, and Peter J. Rentfrow. "Happier People Live More Active Lives: Using Smartphones to Link Happiness and Physical Activity." *PLOS One* 12(1) (Jan. 4, 2017): e0160589.

Lau, Hi Po Bobo, Mathew P. White, and Simone Schnall. "Quantifying the Value of Emotions Using a Willingness to Pay Approach." *Journal of Happiness Studies* 14(5) (Oct. 1, 2013): 1543–61.

Lehrer, Brian. "A 'New World Order When It Comes to Car Safety.'" *The Brian Lehrer Show* (podcast), produced by WNYC. July 13, 2017. http://www .wnyc.org/story/car-safety.

Levine, Amir, and Rachel Heller. *Attached: The New Science of Adult Attachment and How It Can Help You Find—and Keep—Love*. Rpnt. ed. New York: TarcherPerigee, 2012.

Little, Laura M., Debra L. Nelson, J. Craig Wallace, and Paul D. Johnson. "Integrating Attachment Style, Vigor at Work, and Extra-Role Performance." *Journal of Organizational Behavior* 32(3) (Apr. 1, 2011): 464–84.

Lyubomirsky, Sonja. "Hedonic Adaptation to Positive and Negative Experiences." In *The Oxford Handbook of Stress, Health, and Coping*, edited by Susan Folkman. Oxford Handbooks Online. Oxford University Press,

New York, 2010. www.oxfordhandbooks.com/view/10.1093/oxfordhb/9780195375343.001.0001/oxfordhb-9780195375343-e-011.

——. *The How of Happiness*. New York: Penguin Books, 2007.

MacDonald, Geoff, and Terry K. Borsook. "Attachment Avoidance and Feelings of Connection in Social Interaction." *Journal of Experimental Social Psychology* 46(6) (Nov. 2010): 1122–25.

Marlatt, G. Alan, and Judith R. Gordon, eds. *Relapse Prevention: Maintenance Strategies in the Treatment of Addictive Behaviors*. New York: Guilford Press, 1985.

McGonigal, Kelly. *The Willpower Instinct: How Self-Control Works, Why It Matters, and What You Can Do to Get More of It*. New York: Penguin, 2011.

McKay, Matthew, Patrick Fanning, and Patricia E. Zurita Ona. *Mind and Emotions: A Universal Treatment for Emotional Disorders*. Workbook ed. Oakland, CA: New Harbinger, 2011.

Mickelson, Kristin D., Ronald C. Kessler, and Phillip R. Shaver. "Adult Attachment in a Nationally Representative Sample." *Journal of Personality and Social Psychology* 73(5) (Nov. 1997): 1092–1106.

Murray, Sandra L., John G. Holmes, and Dale W. Griffin. "The Self-Fulfilling Nature of Positive Illusions in Romantic Relationships: Love Is Not Blind, but Prescient." *Journal of Personality and Social Psychology* 71(6) (Dec. 1996): 1155–80.

Newby, Jill M., Anna McKinnon, Willem Kuyken, Simon Gilbody, and Tim Dalgleish. "Systematic Review and Meta-Analysis of Transdiagnostic Psychological Treatments for Anxiety and Depressive Disorders in Adulthood." *Clinical Psychology Review* 40 (Aug. 2015): 91–110.

Newman, Michelle G., and Sandra J. Llera. "A Novel Theory of Experiential Avoidance in Generalized Anxiety Disorder: A Review and Synthesis of

Research Supporting a Contrast Avoidance Model of Worry." *Clinical Psychology Review* 31(3) (Apr. 2011): 371–82.

Nickerson, Raymond S. "Confirmation Bias: A Ubiquitous Phenomenon in Many Guises." *Review of General Psychology* 2(2) (Jun. 1998): 175–220.

———. "How We Know—and Sometimes Misjudge—What Others Know: Imputing One's Own Knowledge to Others." *Psychological Bulletin* 125(6) (Nov. 1999): 737–59.

Norem, Julie K., and Edward C. Chang. "The Positive Psychology of Negative Thinking." *Journal of Clinical Psychology* 58(9) (Sept. 2002): 993–1001.

Oaten, Megan, and Ken Cheng. "Longitudinal Gains in Self-Regulation from Regular Physical Exercise." *British Journal of Health Psychology* 11(4) (Nov. 2006): 717–33.

Oettingen, Gabriele, Doris Mayer, and Sam Portnow. "Pleasure Now, Pain Later: Positive Fantasies About the Future Predict Symptoms of Depression." *Psychological Science* 27(3) (Mar. 1, 2016): 345–53.

Overall, Nickola C., Jeffry A. Simpson, and Helena Struthers. "Buffering Attachment-Related Avoidance: Softening Emotional and Behavioral Defenses during Conflict Discussions." *Journal of Personality and Social Psychology* 104(5) (May 2013): 854–71.

Pines, Ayala Malach. "Adult Attachment Styles and Their Relationship to Burnout: A Preliminary, Cross-Cultural Investigation." *Work & Stress* 18(1) (Jan. 1, 2004): 66–80.

Prochaska, James O., and Carlo C. DiClemente. "Transtheoretical Therapy: Toward a More Integrative Model of Change." *Psychotherapy: Theory, Research & Practice* 19(3) (Fall 1982): 276.

Prochaska, James O., Wayne F. Velicer, Joseph S. Rossi, Michael G. Goldstein, Bess H. Marcus, William Rakowski, Christine Fiore, et al. "Stages of

Change and Decisional Balance for 12 Problem Behaviors." *Health Psychology* 13(1) (Jan. 1994): 39.

Pronin, Emily, Daniel Y. Lin, and Lee Ross. "The Bias Blind Spot." *Personality and Social Psychology Bulletin* 28(3) (Mar. 1, 2002): 369–381.

Read, Daniel, and George Loewenstein. "Diversification Bias: Explaining the Discrepancy in Variety Seeking between Combined and Separated Choices." *Journal of Experimental Psychology: Applied* 1(1) (Mar. 1995): 34–49.

Rector, Neil A., R. Michael Bagby, Zindel V. Segal, Russell T. Joffe, and Anthony Levitt. "Self-Criticism and Dependency in Depressed Patients Treated with Cognitive Therapy or Pharmacotherapy." *Cognitive Therapy and Research* 24(5) (Oct. 1, 2000): 571–84.

Richards, Carl. "Overcoming an Aversion to Loss." *The New York Times*, December 9, 2013. http://www.nytimes.com/2013/12/09/your-money /overcoming-an-aversion-to-loss.html.

Rios, Kimberly, Kenneth G. DeMarree, and Johnathan Statzer. "Attitude Certainty and Conflict Style: Divergent Effects of Correctness and Clarity." *Personality and Social Psychology Bulletin* 40(7) (Jul. 1, 2014): 819–30.

Rubin, Gretchen. *Better Than Before: What I Learned About Making and Breaking Habits—To Sleep More, Quit Sugar, Procrastinate Less, and Generally Build a Happier Life*. Rpnt. ed. New York: Broadway Books, 2015.

———. *The Happiness Project: Or, Why I Spent a Year Trying to Sing in the Morning, Clean My Closets, Fight Right, Read Aristotle, and Generally Have More Fun*. Rev. ed. New York: Harper Paperbacks, 2015.

———. "Quiz: Are You an Over-Buyer or an Under-Buyer?" Gretchen Rubin (website). April 22, 2009. http://gretchenrubin.com/happiness_project /2009/04/quiz-are-you-an-overbuyer-or-an-underbuyer.

———. "We Must Have Treats! Here's Why." Gretchen Rubin (website). November 24, 2014. http://gretchenrubin.com/happiness_project/2014/11/we-must-have-treats-heres-why.

———. "Which of These 10 Categories of Loopholes Do You Invoke?" Gretchen Rubin (website). February 5, 2014. http://gretchenrubin.com/happiness_project/2014/02/which-of-these-10-categories-of-loopholes-do-you-invoke.

Saferstein, Jocelyn A., Greg J. Neimeyer, and Chad L. Hagans. "Attachment as a Predictor of Friendship Qualities in College Youth." *Social Behavior and Personality: An International Journal* 33(8) (Jan. 1, 2005): 767–76.

Salkovskis, Paul M. "Obsessional-Compulsive Problems: A Cognitive-Behavioural Analysis." *Behaviour Research and Therapy* 23(5) (Feb. 1985): 571–83.

Schwartz, David J. *The Magic of Thinking Big.* New York: Prentice Hall, 2014.

Shomaker, Lauren B., and Wyndol Furman. "Parent-Adolescent Relationship Qualities, Internal Working Models, and Attachment Styles as Predictors of Adolescents' Interactions with Friends." *Journal of Social and Personal Relationships* 26(5) (Aug. 1, 2009): 579–603.

Stadler, Gertraud, Gabriele Oettingen, and Peter M. Gollwitzer. "Intervention Effects of Information and Self-Regulation on Eating Fruits and Vegetables over Two Years." *Health Psychology* 29(3) (May 2010): 274–83.

———. "Physical Activity in Women: Effects of a Self-Regulation Intervention." *American Journal of Preventive Medicine* 36(1) (Jan. 2009): 29–34.

Startup, H. M., and G. C. L. Davey. "Inflated Responsibility and the Use of Stop Rules for Catastrophic Worrying." *Behaviour Research and Therapy* 41(4) (Apr. 2003): 495–503.

Stone, Douglas, Bruce Patton, Sheila Heen, and Roger Fisher. *Difficult Conversations: How to Discuss What Matters Most.* Updated ed. New York: Penguin Books, 2010.

Tatkin, Stan, and Harville Hendrix. *Wired for Love: How Understanding Your Partner's Brain and Attachment Style Can Help You Defuse Conflict and Build a Secure Relationship.* Oakland, CA: New Harbinger, 2012.

Time Well Spent. "Take Control of Your Phone." http://www.timewellspent .io/take-control/.

Tolin, David F. "Is Cognitive-Behavioral Therapy More Effective Than Other Therapies? A Meta-Analytic Review." *Clinical Psychology Review* 30(6) (Aug. 2010): 710–20.

Towler, Annette J., and Alice F. Stuhlmacher. "Attachment Styles, Relationship Satisfaction, and Well-Being in Working Women." *Journal of Social Psychology* 153(3) (Jun. 2013): 279–98.

Von Haaren, Birte, Joerg Ottenbacher, Julia Muenz, Rainer Neumann, Klaus Boes, and Ulrich Ebner-Priemer. "Does a 20–Week Aerobic Exercise Training Programme Increase Our Capabilities to Buffer Real-Life Stressors? A Randomized, Controlled Trial Using Ambulatory Assessment." *European Journal of Applied Physiology* 116(2) (Feb. 2016): 383–94.

Waters, Everett, Claire E. Hamilton, and Nancy S. Weinfield. "The Stability of Attachment Security from Infancy to Adolescence and Early Adulthood: General Introduction." *Child Development* 71(3) (May 1, 2000): 678–83.

Weinstein, Neil D. "Unrealistic Optimism about Future Life Events." *Journal of Personality and Social Psychology* 39(5) (Nov. 1980): 806–20.

Welch, Ronald D., and Melissa E. Houser. "Extending the Four-Category Model of Adult Attachment: An Interpersonal Model of Friendship Attachment." *Journal of Social and Personal Relationships* 27(3) (Apr. 22, 2010): 351–66.

Wesnousky, Alexandra E., Gabriele Oettingen, and Peter M. Gollwitzer. "Holding a Silver Lining Theory: When Negative Attributes Heighten

Performance." *Journal of Experimental Social Psychology* 57 (Mar. 2015): 15–22.

Wikipedia, s.v. "Big Five Personality Traits." Last modified February 16, 2017. https://en.wikipedia.org/w/index.php?title=Big_Five_personality_traits&oldid=765739426.

Wikipedia, s.v. "False Consensus Effect." Last modified March 11, 2017. https://en.wikipedia.org/w/index.php?title=False_consensus_effect&oldid=769829912.

Wikipedia, s.v. "Premack's Principle." Last modified February 14, 2017. https://en.wikipedia.org/w/index.php?title=Premack%27s_principle&oldid=765363879.

Wilcox, Keith, Beth Vallen, Lauren Block, and Gavan J. Fitzsimons. "Vicarious Goal Fulfillment: When the Mere Presence of a Healthy Option Leads to an Ironically Indulgent Decision." *Journal of Consumer Research* 36(3) (Oct. 1, 2009): 380–93.

Winch, Guy. *Emotional First Aid: Healing Rejection, Guilt, Failure, and Other Everyday Hurts*. Rpnt. ed. New York: Plume, 2014.

You, Hyo Soon, and Kathleen Malley-Morrison. "Young Adult Attachment Styles and Intimate Relationships with Close Friends: A Cross-Cultural Study of Koreans and Caucasian Americans." *Journal of Cross-Cultural Psychology*, 31(4) (Jul. 1, 2000): 528–34.

Zabelina, Darya L., and Michael D. Robinson. "Don't Be So Hard on Yourself: Self-Compassion Facilitates Creative Originality among Self-Judgmental Individuals." *Creativity Research Journal* 22(3) (Aug. 12, 2010): 288–93.

INDEX

. . . .

ABOUT THE AUTHOR

Alice Boyes graduated with her PhD in psychology in 2007. Her doctoral research was about relationships, and it was published in the prestigious *Journal of Personality and Social Psychology*. She worked as a clinical psychologist in her native country, New Zealand, from 2008 until 2013, while also blogging and writing for magazines. She has retired from practice and, careerwise, turned to writing. Her first book, *The Anxiety Toolkit*, was published in 2015. Her blog posts for *Psychology Today* have received over 10 million views. She's Mom to one daughter, born in 2016.

Also by Alice Boyes, PhD

"*The Anxiety Toolkit* provides quick, simple, and practical tips that the anxious person can use now." —**Robert L. Leahy, PhD**, director of the American Institute for Cognitive Therapy

Strategies for
Fine-Tuning
Your Mind and Moving Past
Your Stuck
Points

THE

ANXIETY

TOOLKIT

ALICE BOYES, PhD